The "Unemployed Workmen Act, 1905" : with the orders and regulations issued by the local government board under the provisions of the Act, and notes.

The "Unemployed Workmen Act, 1905" : with the orders and regulations issued by the local government board under the provisions of the Act, and notes.
Multiple Contributors, See Notes
collection ID CTRG97-B1269
Reproduction from York University Law School Library
Includes index.
Rochdale : Local Government Printing and Pub. Co., 1905.
192 p. : forms ; 16 cm

The Making of Modern Law collection of legal archives constitutes a genuine revolution in historical legal research because it opens up a wealth of rare and previously inaccessible sources in legal, constitutional, administrative, political, cultural, intellectual, and social history. This unique collection consists of three extensive archives that provide insight into more than 300 years of American and British history. These collections include:

Legal Treatises, 1800-1926: over 20,000 legal treatises provide a comprehensive collection in legal history, business and economics, politics and government.

Trials, 1600-1926: nearly 10,000 titles reveal the drama of famous, infamous, and obscure courtroom cases in America and the British Empire across three centuries.

Primary Sources, 1620-1926: includes reports, statutes and regulations in American history, including early state codes, municipal ordinances, constitutional conventions and compilations, and law dictionaries.

These archives provide a unique research tool for tracking the development of our modern legal system and how it has affected our culture, government, business – nearly every aspect of our everyday life. For the first time, these high-quality digital scans of original works are available via print-on-demand, making them readily accessible to libraries, students, independent scholars, and readers of all ages.

old books. new life.

The BiblioLife Network

This project was made possible in part by the BiblioLife Network (BLN), a project aimed at addressing some of the huge challenges facing book preservationists around the world. The BLN includes libraries, library networks, archives, subject matter experts, online communities and library service providers. We believe every book ever published should be available as a high-quality print reproduction; printed on-demand anywhere in the world. This insures the ongoing accessibility of the content and helps generate sustainable revenue for the libraries and organizations that work to preserve these important materials.

The following book is in the "public domain" and represents an authentic reproduction of the text as printed by the original publisher. While we have attempted to accurately maintain the integrity of the original work, there are sometimes problems with the original work or the micro-film from which the books were digitized. This can result in minor errors in reproduction. Possible imperfections include missing and blurred pages, poor pictures, markings and other reproduction issues beyond our control. Because this work is culturally important, we have made it available as part of our commitment to protecting, preserving, and promoting the world's literature.

GUIDE TO FOLD-OUTS MAPS and OVERSIZED IMAGES

The book you are reading was digitized from microfilm captured over the past thirty to forty years. Years after the creation of the original microfilm, the book was converted to digital files and made available in an online database.

In an online database, page images do not need to conform to the size restrictions found in a printed book. When converting these images back into a printed bound book, the page sizes are standardized in ways that maintain the detail of the original. For large images, such as fold-out maps, the original page image is split into two or more pages

Guidelines used to determine how to split the page image follows:

• Some images are split vertically; large images require vertical and horizontal splits.
• For horizontal splits, the content is split left to right.
• For vertical splits, the content is split from top to bottom.
• For both vertical and horizontal splits, the image is processed from top left to bottom right.

THE

"Unemployed Workmen Act, 1905."

With the Orders and Regulations issued by the
Local Government Board under the Provisions
of the Act; and Notes

BY

R. A. LEACH,

OF GRAY'S INN, BARRISTER-AT-LAW,

Author of "Education of Pauper Children." "Criticism and Analysis of Valuation
Bill, 1904." Joint-Author of the "Vaccination Law," &c.

———

1905.
LOCAL GOVERNMENT PRINTING AND PUBLISHING COMPANY,
ROCHDALE.

PREFACE.

In the preparation of this work my only aim has been to produce a handbook of ready and complete assistance to all who collectively or individually have anything to do with the carrying out of the provisions of the Unemployed Workmen Act, 1905, and the Orders and Regulations issued by the Local Government Board under the provisions of the Act.

Nothing has been left out of the book that was thought would be of any service, especially to members of Distress Committees and Central Bodies and their officers. Instead of giving altogether the circular letters sent out by the Local Government Board, on the issue of their Orders and Regulations, I have purposely adopted the plan of making all the necessary extracts from such letters and using them in the notes to the sections of the Act or the Articles of the Orders and Regulations to which such extracts particularly relate. This plan yields the advantage of getting the opinions and suggestions of the Board in the places most convenient to all who, using the book, desire to have at sight any opinion or suggestion that the Local Government Board may have given or made upon any particular point.

The book has been got out under pressure of time. Great care, nevertheless, has been taken to have its contents as correct as possible; the first three lines of note (3) on page 45, however, should be read with the more correctly worded statement on page 8 of the Introduction.

I here desire to express my thanks to Mr. H. W. Fordham, Superintendent of the "London Unemployed Fund Central Labour Exchange" for the labour exchange rules and forms given in the book; also to Mr. A. H. Lionel Leach, of Gray's Inn, and to Mr. R. Webber Leach, of Gray's Inn, for the assistance they have been to me in the preparation of the work.

October, 1905.   R.A.L.

————◆————

TABLE OF CONTENTS.

ABBREVIATIONS IN NOTES.
"L.G.B.C.L." Local Government Board Circular Letter.

INTRODUCTION.

"The Unemployed Workmen Act, 1905," is, undoubtedly, the outcome of a widespread demand that some statutory provision should be made, apart from the poor law, for the distressed unemployed. The demand has grown in intensity during recent years, and after the inauguration of the voluntary organisation of the scheme known as the "London Unemployed Fund"—a scheme which had its origin in proposals laid before a Conference of Metropolitan Guardians by the Right Hon. W. H. Long, M.P., then President of the Local Government Board, on October 14th, 1904—it was, very naturally, expected that the speech from the Throne at the opening of the 1905 Session of Parliament would disclose the Government's intention to introduce legislation for the establishment, not only in London but also in the provinces, of organisation for the aid of the unemployed in proper cases. The expectation was not unjustified. The King's speech contained the following gracious words :—

"Legislation will be submitted to you for the establish-
"ment of authorities to deal with the question of the unemployed.
"I have noticed, with profound regret and sympathy, the ab-
"normal distress which has been caused by the want of

"employment during the present winter. Arrangements of a
"temporary character have been made to meet the difficulty,
"but it is expedient now to provide machinery for this purpose
"of a more permanent character."

Accordingly, on the 18th April, the President of the
Local Government Board (Mr. Gerald Balfour, M.P.) introduced
the promised Measure in the House of Commons.

DIFFERENCES BETWEEN ORIGINAL BILL AND ACT.

The Act in several important respects is very different
from the Bill originally introduced.

The provisions of the Bill for the constitution of Distress
Committees and Central Bodies differed from the present Act in
that :—(1) The power to co-opt additional members was optional,
and thus, if this had been so left by the Act, the Distress Committees might have been constituted entirely of members of the
Borough Councils and Board of Guardians, and Central Bodies
of members of such Committees; (2) co-opted members were not
necessarily to be chosen from persons "experienced in the relief
of distress"; (3) no power was given to the Local Government
Board to appoint other additional members to Central Bodies;
(4) the Distress Committees outside London, with power and
duties of Central Bodies [Act, Section 2 (1)] were only to be

established in County Boroughs, and the establishment might be postponed in any such Borough on representation made by the Borough Council to the Local Government Board. It was proposed in respect of provincial administrative county areas that organisation on London lines (*i.e.*, Distress Committees and Central Bodies) should be established on application to the Local Government Board, but there was no proposal in the Bill for the Board to have power to establish, without request, in any such area, on deeming it expedient, any such organisation. By a reference to sections 1 (1) and 2 of the Act it will be at once seen how very different the provisions of the Act for the establishment of organisation are to the provisions of the original Bill. They are alike in respect of the Special Committees *re* Labour Exchanges.

The original Bill applied only to England and Wales; the Act not only applies to England and Wales but also to Scotland [Section 5] and Ireland [Section 6].

The original Bill contained no time limit. The duration of the Act is limited to three years from its date (11th August, 1905) unless Parliament otherwise determine [Section 8].

Two proposals in the original Bill which gave rise to considerable discussion in the House of Commons do not appear in the Act. They were (1) a provision "that the total weekly remuneration given for any temporary work so provided " (*i.e.,* *under the Act*) should be "less than that which would under ordinary circumstances be earned by an unskilled labourer for a full week's work, and, except with the consent of the Local Government Board, temporary work" should not "be so provided for the same person in more than two successive years"; and (2) "For the purposes of this Section work" was to be deemed to be provided by a Body established under this Act (although the workman was not actually employed by that Body), if that Body had "arranged for the employment of the workman and contributed towards the payment given in respect of that employment." Although these two clauses of the original Bill are not in the Act, it will be found on reference to the Local Government Board's " Regulations (Organisation for Unemployed) 1905 " [Articles V. and II. (1) (iv.) (*d*)] that the Local Government Board under their delegated legislative authority [Section 4 (3) (*a*)] have actually or in effect imposed them.

The proposal in the original Bill to allow expenses of providing temporary work at Farm Colonies out of contributions from Councils is not in the Act, the application of such contributions being restricted by Section 1 (6) in such a way as permits of no wages being paid out of such contributions for unemployed provided with work under the Act.

In some respects the Act is less generous than the original Bill, in others more generous. The provisions of the Act and the original Bill are identical in respect of the class of unemployed who may be assisted, but the Act makes larger provisions in respect of the character of assistance that may be given. The Bill made provision for aiding the migration or emigration of an unemployed workman but not for any of his dependants. The Act does both [Section 1 (5)].

The original Bill made no provision for the temporary accommodation for persons for whom work upon the land is provided. The Act does [Section 4 (3) (*b*)]. Owing, however, to the restrictions made by Section 1 (6) the contributions from Councils cannot be used to provide such accommodation. On this, however, see Note (1) pp. 118-119.

THE ACT THE OUTCOME OF CONCESSIONS.

It would scarcely be expected that any measure introduced to Parliament, for affording, at the expense of the Rates, provision, apart from the Poor Law, for the distressed unemployed, would become law with the ready accord of all our legislators. Although the origin of the Bill was to be found in the origin of the "London Unemployed Fund" mentioned above, it soon became evident that the measure was objectionable to legislators who, though equal in sympathy with the deserving unemployed, were politically as wide apart as possible. On the one hand the measure was far too meagre to satisfy Labour Members;

on the other hand it was looked upon by a large number of
Ministerialists as being of an exceedingly mischievous nature.
Indeed, it would be hard to find any government measure
that was so contrary to the voiced views of Ministerialists
as this measure was.   Notwithstanding the statement of
the President of the Local Government Board, on the
second reading of the Bill in the House of Commons
[June 20th], that in the opinion of the Government it was
not wise at the stage we had reached to have recourse to a
single *non possumus*, or to interpose a mere dam or barrier in the
way of public opinion instead of endeavouring to guide it into
channels which should lead to the least harm, and be most
likely to be fruitful of good [Parliamentary Debates], it is very
questionable if the measure would have been passed in any shape
but for two things, viz.:—(1) The amended proposals of the
Government on the Bill reaching the Committee stage in the
House of Commons [August 4th]; and (2) The Government's
promise announced by the Prime Minister in that House [August
2nd] of the appointment of a Royal Commission to (1) survey
everything which appertained to dealing with the problem of the
poor, whether poor by their own fault or by temporary lack of
employment, and (2) to investigate what means could be taken
to deal with problems which thus arose, whether by employment
by municipalities or in any other way.   It was thought that such
a commission would be able to complete their labours within
three years, and therefore that the duration of the proposed
Unemployment Act might be limited to such a period.   To these
concessions the passage of the measure may be credited.

THE LABOUR ACT, 1832.

It is of interest to note that, on the appointment of the Royal Commission on Poor Laws in 1832, a temporary "Labour Act" (2 and 3 Will. IV., c. 96) was passed. The Act was "For the better employment of labourers in agricultural parishes until the 25th March, 1834." In its opening recital it was stated that, notwithstanding the many laws in force for the relief and employment of the poor, many able-bodied labourers were frequently entirely destitute of work or unprofitably employed, and in many instances received insufficient allowance for their support from the Poor Rates; also that the mode of providing employment for the poor, which might be expedient in some parishes, might be inexpedient in others, and that it might therefore be desirable to extend the powers of parish vestries, in order that such a course might be pursued as best adapted to the peculiar circumstances of each. The limit of its duration to two years was because it was thought that in two years the country would be in possession of the Report of the Royal Commission. This seems an all sufficient precedent for limiting the duration of the present Act to three years, in which time the new Royal Commission should be able to finally report.

THE PRESENT ACT NOT INTENDED TO SOLVE THE PROBLEM OF THE UNEMPLOYED.

The present Act is not intended to solve the unemployed problem. The President of the Local Government Board (Mr. Gerald Balfour, M.P.) in moving the second reading of the Bill, said that:—

"The present Bill did not pretend to deal with the whole "of the vast and complicated problem known as the unem-

" ployed question, it did not attempt to do more than deal with
" a part, not altogether an unimportant part, but only a part of
" that problem, and any attempt to extend its principle to the
" whole field of unemployment would be foredoomed to disastrous
" failure. Anybody reading the text of the Bill with attention
" would see that the object throughout was to assist only a
" limited class of the unemployed, and even as regarded appli-
" cants of that class it was not intended that there should be any
" kind of obligation to find work for them, as was thrown on
" Guardians to provide relief in cases of destitution. The limited
" class of the unemployed was defined in Sub-clause 3 of
" Clause 1 of the Bill as—' Honestly desirous of obtaining work,
" but temporarily unable to do so from exceptional causes over
" which the applicant has no control.'

      " And the limitation was extended to cases which, in the
" opinion of the local body to whom application is made, are
" . 'Capable of more suitable treatment under this Act than
" under the poor law.' He wanted the House to understand the
" full significence of the definition—the desire was to exclude
" loafers, work-shyers, intermittent workers whose case was not
" exceptional, and any workman out of work from fault of his
" own. The exact interpretation of the words—'Capable of
" more suitable treatment than under the poor law '—would,
" of course, depend on the general provisions of the Bill and the
" Regulations to be made by the Local Government Board under
" Clause 4, and such Regulations would include rules which
" would exclude distress not due to lack of employment, chronic
" distress, applicants of bad character, applicants not complying
" with conditions of residence, preference being given to work-
" men with established homes and with wives and families "
[Parliamentary Debates].

An examination of the Local Government Board's Regulations made under the Act, show that apart from the benefits that may be afforded by Labour Exchanges, only the better or best class of the distressed unemployed will receive any benefit from the present Act. Besides, if the new Bodies constituted for dealing with the better or best class of unemployed act on the suggestion of the Local Government Board, the benefits will be only obtainable in periods of exceptional distress.

THE ADVANTAGES AFFORDED BY THE ACT.

Notwithstanding the limitations made by the Act and the Regulations, the measure is far from being the sham that some have termed it. Even if voluntary subscriptions are not [see Section 1 (6) of the Act], as many fear, sufficient to enable the new Bodies, organised to administer the provisions of the Act, to enter upon any large Undertakings, such as Farm Colonies, or the reclamation of waste land, or the making or improvement of highways, yet the Organisation established should prove exceedingly useful to the Councils in large Urban Areas. Because of the restriction on amount and application of the contributions from Rates [Section 1 (6)], these Bodies are, as winters come, certain to be pressed to enter themselves on Undertakings as many have done in winters for years past for the benefit of the unemployed. The present Act may not stop them from doing so again. If, therefore, any such works for the reason given are entered upon, it will be found a great advantage to have at hand an organisation which should prove useful in weeding out the unemployable and the undeserving from the employable deserving. Again the provision in the Act and Regulations under which Labour Exchanges may be established—if properly worked and the same Bodies co-operate, as they may—throughout the whole country is a substantial advantage when taken with the provision for aiding, out of Rate contributions, migration from districts where there is a superabundance of workers to districts where there is a scarcity. Organised trades practically have their own labour registers, but unorganised workers have not. The emigration provisions are not, by reason of the restrictions on the contributions from rates, as liberal as the poor law emigration provisions, but the provision for aiding migration is one that meets a shortage in the Poor Law Acts. Finally, the best class of distressed unemployed man or woman —for the provisions include women as well as men—can have such aid as the Act, with the Regulations, provides, without the drawback of that loss of civil rights [Section 1 (7)] which non-medical poor law relief involve. This last-named advantage seems to be in accord with the public conscience.

FULL TEXT OF THE

UNEMPLOYED WORKMEN ACT, 1905.

[5 Edw. 7.   Ch. 18.]

ARRANGEMENT OF SECTIONS.

B

CHAPTER XVIII.

An Act to establish organisation with a view to the
provision of Employment or Assistance for Unemployed Workmen in proper cases.

[11th August, 1905.]

BE it enacted by the King's most Excellent Majesty,
by and with the advice and consent of the Lords
Spiritual and Temporal, and Commons, in this present
Parliament assembled, and by the authority of the
same, as follows :—

Organi-
sation for
London.

1. (1) For the purposes of this Act there shall be
established, by order of the Local Government Board
under this Act, a distress committee of the council of
every metropolitan borough in London, consisting
partly of members of the borough council and partly
of members of the board of guardians of every poor
law union wholly or partly within the borough and of
persons experienced in the relief of distress, and a
central body for the whole of the administrative county
of London, consisting partly of members of, and selected
by, the distress committees and of members of, and
selected by, the London County Council, and partly of
persons co-opted to be additional members of the body,
and partly, if the order so provides, of persons nominated by the Local Government Board, but the number
of the persons so co-opted and nominated shall not

exceed one-fourth of the total number of the body, and every such order shall provide that one member at least of the committee or body established by the order shall be a woman.

Note.—S. 1 (1) For the Order of the Local Government Board establishing Distress Committees and Central Body in London, see "The Organisation (Unemployed Workmen) Establishment Order, 1905."

(2) The distress committee shall make themselves acquainted with the conditions of labour within their area, and when so required by the central body shall receive, inquire into, and discriminate between any applications made to them from persons unemployed:

Provided that a distress committee shall not entertain an application from any person unless they are satisfied that he has resided in London for such period, not being less than twelve months, immediately before the application, as the central body fix as a residential qualification.

(3) If the distress committee are satisfied that any such applicant is honestly desirous of obtaining work, but is temporarily unable to do so from exceptional causes over which he has no control, and consider that his case is capable of more suitable treatment under this Act than under the poor law, they may endeavour to obtain work for the applicant, or, if they think the case is one for treatment by the central body rather than by themselves, refer the case to the central body, but the distress committee shall have no power to

provide, or contribute towards the provision of, work for any unemployed person.

NOTE.—S. 1 (2) and (3) For duties of the Distress Committee and the conditions affecting applications to the Committee, and cases referred to Central Body, see Section 4 (3) (*a*) and Article II. of "The Regulations (Organisation for Unemployed), 1905."

(4) The central body shall superintend and, as far as possible, co-ordinate the action of the distress committees, and aid the efforts of those committees by establishing, taking over, or assisting labour exchanges and employment registers, and by the collection of information and otherwise as they think fit.

NOTE —S. 1 (4). See Section 4 (3) (*a*) and Article XIX. of "The Regulations (Organisation for Unemployed), 1905."

(5) The central body may, if they think fit, in any case of an unemployed person referred to them by a distress committee, assist that person by aiding the emigration or removal to another area of that person and any of his dependants, or by providing, or contributing towards the provision of, temporary work in such manner as they think best calculated to put him in a position to obtain regular work or other means of supporting himself.

NOTE.—S. 1 (5). See Section 4 (3) (*a*) for the conditions under which emigration may be aided see Article III. of "The Regulations (Organisation for Unemployed), 1905."

On the conditions under which removal to another area may be aided see Article IV. of said Regulations.

For the conditions under which assistance in the form of Temporary Work may be given see Article V. of the said Regulations.

(6) Any expenses of the central body under this Act, and such of the expenses of the distress committees under this Act as are incurred with the consent of the central body, shall be defrayed out of a central fund under the management of the central body, which shall be supplied by voluntary contributions given for the purpose, and by contributions made on the demand of the central body by the council of each metropolitan borough in proportion to the rateable value of the borough and paid as part of the expenses of the council:

Provided that—

(*a*) A separate account shall be kept of all sums supplied by contributions made by the councils of the metropolitan boroughs, and no expenses except—

(i.) establishment charges of the central body and the distress committees, including the expenses incurred by them in respect of labour exchanges and employment registers and in the collection of information; and

(ii.) the expenses incurred by the central body in aiding the emigration or removal to another area of an unemployed person and any of his dependants; and

(iii.) the expenses incurred by the central body in relation to the acquisition, with the consent of the Local Government Board, of land for the purposes of this Act;

shall be paid out of that account.

(*b*) No such contribution by a council shall in
any year exceed the amount which would be
produced by a rate of one halfpenny in the
pound calculated on the whole rateable value
of the borough, or such higher rate, not
exceeding one penny, as the Local Government Board may approve.

NOTE.—S. 1 (6). See Section 4 (3), (*c*), and Article XIV. o
"The Regulations (Organisation for Unemployed) 1905" as to
acceptance of donations.

See Section 4 (3), (*b*), (*e*), (*h*), and Articles VIII., IX., X.,
and XVIII. of the said Regulations as to (1) establishment of
Farm Colony; (2) Temporary Accommodation for persons at
work; (3) Acquisition of Land; and (4) Borrowing Powers,
respectively.

See Section 4 (3), (*h*), and Article XVII. of the said
Regulations as to Rate Contributions.

See Section (4), (3), (*f*), and Article XV. of the said
Regulations as to transfer of receipts of Farm Colony to
Voluntary Contribution Account.

See Section 4 (3), (*g*), and Article XVI. of the said
Regulations as to how Accounts are to be made up and audited.

In the London Government Act, 1899 (62 and 63 Vic.,
c. 14 s. 34) the expression "Rateable Value" includes the
value "of Government Property upon which a contribution in
lieu of Rates is paid."

(7) The provision of temporary work or other
assistance for any person under this Act shall not
disentitle him to be registered or to vote as a parliamentary, county, or parochial elector, or as a burgess.

NOTE.—S. 1 (7) There are a number of precedents for the
preserving of the franchise to persons assisted under the Act.
Amongst such it may be mentioned that under "The Elementary
Education Act, 1876 (39 and 40 Vict. c. 79), Section 10. Where
a non-pauper parent by reason of poverty is unable to pay the
ordinary school fees for his children, such fees may be paid by
the Guardians of the Poor. The Section provides that "the
parent shall not, by reason of any payment under this Section,
be deprived of any franchise, right or privilege, or be subject

Sect. 1.

to any disability or disqualification." A similar provision is contained in respect of cost of education, including maintenance of a blind and deaf child under the provisions of "The Elementary Education (Blind and Deaf Children) Act, 1893 (56 and 57 Vict. c. 42), Sect. 10, and "The Elementary Education (Defective and Epileptic Children) Act, 1899," (62 and 63 Vict. c. 32), Sect. 8 (2) "The Municipal Corporations Act, 1882 (45 and 46 Vic. c. 50. Sect. 33 (4) enacts "a person shall not be disentitled to be enrolled as a burgess by reason only—(a) that he has received medical or surgical assistance from the trustees of the municipal charities, or has been removed by order of a justice to a hospital, or place for reception of the sick, at the cost of any local authority; or (b) that his child has been admitted to, and taught in any public or endowed school." See further "The Vaccination Act, 1867" (30 and 31 Vic. c. 84) s. 26; "The Medical Relief Disqualification and Removal Act, 1885" (48 and 49 Vic. c. 46); "The Public Health (in London) Act, 1891" (54 and 55 Vic. c. 76) s. 80 (4); "The Isolation Hospitals Act, 1893" (56 and 57 Vic. c. 68) s. 23; "The Cleansing of the Persons Act, 1897" (60 and 61 Vic. c. 31) s. 1.

(8) This section shall apply to the City of London as if the City of London were a metropolitan borough, and the mayor, aldermen, and commons of the city of London in common council assembled were the council of the borough, and any contribution required for the purposes of this Act shall be paid out of the consolidated rate, but shall not be reckoned in calculating the amount of the rate for the purpose of any limit on that amount.

(9) The Local Government Board may, upon the application of the council of any borough or district adjoining or near to London, by order, extend the provisions of this section to that borough or district as if the borough or district were a metropolitan borough and were within the administrative county of London, and with such other modifications and adaptations as to the Board may appear necessary.

Organisation outside London.

2. (1) There shall be established by order of the Local Government Board for each municipal borough and urban district with a population, according to the last census for the time being, of not less than fifty thousand, and not being a borough or district to which the provisions of section one of this Act have been extended, a distress committee of the council for the purposes of this Act, with a similar constitution to that of a distress committee in London, and the distress committee so established shall, as regards their borough or district, have the same duties and powers, so far as applicable, as are given by this Act to the distress committees and central body in London.

This provision shall extend to any municipal borough or urban district with a population, according to the last census for the time being, of less than fifty thousand but not less than ten thousand, if the council of the borough or district make an application for the purpose to the Local Government Board, and the Board consent.

(2) Subject as aforesaid, the Local Government Board may, on the application of any county or borough or district council, or board of guardians, or, if they think it expedient, without any such application, by order establish for the purposes of this Act in any county or part of a county a central body and distress committees with similar constitutions to those of the central body and distress committees in London, and the body and committees so established shall, subject to any exceptions made by the order, have the

same duties and powers as respects their area as are given by this Act to the central body and distress committees respectively in London.

For the purposes of this provision a county borough with a population of less than fifty thousand shall be deemed to be included in the county in which it is, for the purposes of the Local Government Act, 1888, deemed to be situated.

51 & 52 Vict. c. 41.

NOTE.—S. 2 (2) In the sub-section it should be understood that (1) County Council means a Council of an Administrative County for which a County Council is elected in pursuance of the Local Government Act, 1888 (51 and 52 Vic. c. 41), S.s. 1 and 100. (2) Borough Council means any place for the time being subject to the Municipal Corporations Act, 1882 (Interpretation Act, 1889—52 and 53 Vic. c. 63, S. 15 (1) (4) (3) District Council means a Council of any Urban or Rural District elected in pursuance of the Local Government Act, 1894 (56 and 57 Vic. c. 73), S.s. 23 and 24; and (4) Board of Guardians means a Board of Guardians elected under the Poor Law Amendment Act, 1834 (4 and 5 Will. IV., c. 76), and the Acts amending the same, and includes a Board of Guardians or other Body of Persons performing under any Local Act the like functions to a Board of Guardians under the Poor Law Amendment Act, 1834 (Interpretation Act, 1889—52 and 53 Vic. c. 63, S. 16 (1).

The power given in the Section to the Local Government Board to establish Distress Committees in any area to which the Sub-Section applies was strongly objected to during the Committee stage in both House of Commons and House of Lords on the grounds that the Local Authorities knew the needs of their respective districts infinitely better than could be known by the Local Government Board, and that to give the Local Government Board such power was inconsistent with the rights of Local Governing Bodies. In answer to such objection the President of the Local Government Board (Mr. Gerald Balfour, M.P.), said that it had been represented to him that the Unemployed in County Districts where the organisation was not in operation might flock into Industrial Districts where it was in operation. He did not think it was a very serious risk, but he was sure the Board would not use this power unless there were very real reasons for so doing. It would be very difficult to force Local Authorities in opposition to their views (Parliamentary Debates).

The following are County Boroughs with populations of less than 50,000:—Bath, Canterbury, Chester, Dudley, Exeter, Gloucester, Lincoln, Oxford, Worcester.

(3) Where a central body and distress committees have not been established under this Act for the whole of a county, the council of that county, and, where a distress committee has not been established under this Act for a county borough, the council of that county borough, shall constitute a special committee under this Act, consisting of members of the council, with power to co-opt any persons to be additional members of the committee; but the number of persons so co-opted shall not exceed one-fourth of the total number of the committee.

It shall be the duty of the council, in such a case, through the special committee, to collect information with respect to the conditions of labour within their area by establishing, taking over, or assisting labour exchanges and employment registers, and in such other manner as they think fit, and to supply any such information when required.

Any expenses incurred by a council under this provision shall be paid in the case of a county council out of the county fund as expenses for special or general county purposes, as the circumstances may require, and in the case of a borough council out of the borough fund or borough rate.

Sect. 2.

Note.—S. 2. (3) The Local Government Board state :—At present a Central Body and Distress Committees have not been established for the whole of any county except London, nor has a Distress Committee been established for any County Borough with a population according to the last census of less than 50,000. Consequently under Section 2 (3) of the Act it will be incumbent on every County Council except the London County Council, and on the Council of every County Borough with a population according to the last census of less than 50,000, to constitute a Special Committee under the Act consisting of members of the Council with power to co-opt any persons to be additional members of the Committee. The number of persons so co-opted, however, must not exceed one-fourth of the total number of the Committee. The Council should proceed to appoint a Special Committee in pursuance of the requirements of the Sub-Section " (L.G.B.C.L. 10th October, 1905).

It will be noticed that as regards Distress Committees for County Boroughs that Section 2 (1) requires Distress Committees to be established in such Boroughs with a population of not less than 50,000. "The Urban Distress Committees (Unemployed Workmen) Order, 1905"—Provincial Order—makes provision accordingly, and therefore the expression "County Borough" in Sub-Section 3 should be taken to apply to County Boroughs with a population less than 50,000.

As to duties of Special Committee *re* Labour Exchanges, &c. see "The Regulations (Organisation for Unemployed) 1905" Article XIX.

Sub-Section (3) does not define the area for which a Special Committee are to act in the areas of an Administrative County, but it is submitted that the intention is that the County Council or County Borough shall appoint a Committee for such districts or district in their respective areas in which no organisation is established under Sub-Section 1 or Sub-Section 2 of Section 2.

On the question of expenses the Local Government Board state :—" Any expenses incurred by the Council under the Act must be paid in the case of a County Council out of the County as expenses for special or general county purposes as the circumstances may require, and in the case of a Borough Council out of the borough fund or borough rate. If the whole County is within the area of the Special Committee, the expenses of the County Council should be regarded as general expenses. If, however, only part of the County is within this area, it appears to the Board that the expenses of the Council should be treated as special expenses in that area." L.G.B.C.L., 10th October, 1905.

Sect. 2.

(4) Where any order is made under this section as respects any area, the provisions of this Act relating to London shall apply with respect to that area, with such necessary modifications and adaptations as may be made by the order.

Section 2 (4) see "The Regulations (Organisation for Unemployed) 1905," Article XXI.

Temporary provision pending establishment of proper organisation.

3. Where at any time a central body and distress committees or a distress committee are about to be established for any area under this Act, any body already established in that area, whether before or after the passing of this Act, for the purpose of dealing with the unemployed, and any special committee under this Act, may, if the Local Government Board think fit, be temporarily constituted by order of that Board a central body or a distress committee, as the case may be, until the establishment in accordance with this Act of a central body and distress committees or of a distress committee for that area.

Note.—S. 3. A Body established for dealing with the Unemployed, but not established under Section 1 (1), or Section 2 (1) (2) of the Act, or a Special Committee constituted under Section 2 (5), would not, pending the establishment of organisation under the Section 1 (1) or Section 2 (1) (2) have any status as a "Central Body" or "Distress Committee" under the Act unless constituted as such by a Special Order issued by the Local Government Board, under the provisions in Section 3. See Sect. 4 *re* Transfer of Liabilities, &c.

Local Government Board orders and regulations.

4. (1) An order of the Local Government Board under this Act establishing a central body or distress committee may provide for the constitution and proceedings of that body or committee, and, in the case of an order establishing a central body, for the incorpor-

ation of that body by an appropriate name, and, where any property or liabilities are taken over from any other body, for effecting by virtue of the order the transfer of that property or those liabilities, and also for any matter for which provision may be made by regulations under this Act, and for which it appears desirable to make special provision effecting only the body or committee established by the order.

NOTE.—S. 4 (1) empowers the Local Government Board, in an Order establishing a Central Body or Distress Committee, to make provision, "where any property or liabilities are taken over from any other body, for effecting by virtue of the Order the transfer of the property or those liabilities." No such provision is made in either "The Organisation (Unemployed Workmen) Establishment Order, 1905"—London Order,—or "The Urban Distress Committees (Unemployed Workmen) Order, 1905"—Provincial Order.

Article VI. (1) of "The Organisation (Unemployed Workmen) Order 1905" provides, that the Central Body in London shall be a Body Corporate by the name of Central Employment Body for London, and invest such Central Body with the rights and liability of a Corporate Body. Such a provision is not made in the "Urban Distress Committees (Unemployed Workmen) Order 1905" issued to provincial Boroughs and Urban Districts of not less than 50,000. Provision, however, is made in "The Regulations (Organisation for Unemployed) 1905" for a Distress Committee, established under Section 2 of the Act, to purchase by agreement or take on lease land for the purposes of the Act on consent of the Local Government Board. See Articles X., and XXI. of the said Regulations.

(2) An order of the Local Government Board under this Act may be varied and revoked by any subsequent order of the Board made under this Act.

(3) The Local Government Board may make regulations for carrying into effect this Act, and may by those regulations, amongst other things, provide—

(a) for regulating, subject to the provisions of this Act, the conditions under which any application may be entertained by a distress committee under this Act, and the conditions under which a central body may aid emigration or removal, or provide or contribute towards the provision of work under this Act, and otherwise for regulating the manner in which any duties under this Act are to be performed or powers exercised by any central body or distress committee or special committee under this Act; and

Note.—S. 4 (3), (a) See " Regulations (Organisation for Unemployed) 1905." Articles II., III., IV., and V

(b) for authorising the establishment, with the consent of the Local Government Board, of farm colonies by a central body established under this Act, and the provision, with the like consent, by such a body of temporary accommodation for persons for whom work upon the land is provided; and

Note.—S. 4 (3), (b) See " Regulations (Organisation for Unemployed) 1905." Articles VIII., and IX.

(c) for authorising and regulating the acquisition by a central body of land by agreement for the purposes of this Act, and the disposal of any land so acquired; and

Note.—S. 4 (3), (c) See " Regulations (Organisation for Unemployed) 1905." Articles X., and XXI.

(d) for the employment of officers and provision of offices, and for enabling any inspector of

Sect. 4.

the Local Government Board to attend the
meeting of any body or committee established
under this Act; and

NOTE.—S. 4 (3), (*d*) See "Regulations (Organisation for
Unemployed) 1905." Articles XI., XII. and XIII.

(*e*) for authorising the acceptance of any money
or property by a central body established
under this Act, and for regulating the
administration of any money or property so
acquired; and

NOTE.—S. 4 (3), (*e*) See "Regulations (Organisation for
Unemployed) 1905." Article XIV.

(*f*) for the payment of any receipts of a central
body to the central fund, and for the apportionment, if necessary, of those receipts
between the voluntary contribution account
and the rate contribution account of that
fund; and

NOTE.—S. 4 (3), (*f*) See "Regulations (Organisation for
Unemployed) 1905." Article XV.

(*g*) for the audit of the accounts of any central
body established under this Act in the same
manner and subject to the same provisions
as to any matters incidental to the audit or
consequential thereon as the accounts of a
county council; and

NOTE.—S. 4 (3) (*g*) See "Regulations (Organisation for
Unemployed) 1905." Article XVI.

(*h*) for enforcing the payment of contributions by
any councils liable to make such contributions
in pursuance of this Act, and for authorising

and regulating the borrowing of money by a
central body established under this Act; and

Note.—S. 4 (3), (*h*) See "Regulations (Organisation for
Unemployed) 1905." Articles XVII. and XVIII.

(*i*) for facilitating the co-operation of any body
or committee having powers under this Act
for any area with any other body or committee, or with any local authority, and the
provision of assistance by one such body or
committee to another; and

Note.—S. 4 (3), (*i*) See "Regulations (Organisation for
Unemployed) 1905." Article XX.

(*k*) for applying, with the necessary adaptations,
to a distress committee having the powers
of a central body regulations relating to a
central body; and

Note. S. 4 (3), (*k*) See "Regulations (Organisation for
Unemployed) 1905." Article XXI.

(*l*) for the holding of local inquiries by the Local
Government Board for the purposes of this
Act, and for requiring returns to be made to
the Board by any body or committee having
powers under this Act; and

Note.—S. 4 (3), (*l*) See "Regulations (Organisation for
Unemployed) 1905." Article XXII.

(*m*) for the application for the purposes of this
Act, as respects any matters to be dealt with
by the regulations, of any provision in any
Act of Parliament dealing with the like
matters, with any necessary modifications or
adaptations.

Note. S. 4 (3), (*m*) See "Regulations (Organisation for
Unemployed) 1905." Articles X., XVI., XVII., XVIII. & XXII.

Sect. 4.

All regulations made under this Act shall be laid as soon as may be before Parliament.

5. In the application of this Act to Scotland— Application to Scotland.

   (1) "The Local Government Board for Scotland" shall be substituted for "the Local Government Board":

NOTE.—The Orders and Regulations of the Local Government Board, included in this book, only applying to England and Wales, it has not been thought necessary to annotate anything relating to Scotland or Ireland.

   (2) "Royal, parliamentary, or police burgh" shall be substituted for "municipal borough and urban district" and for "borough or district":

   (3) "Parish" shall be substituted for "poor law union," "parish council" shall be substituted for "board of guardians," and "town council" shall be substituted for "council of the borough or district" and for "borough or district council":

   (4) "Royal, parliamentary, or police burgh with "a population, according to the last census "for the time being, of less than fifty "thousand, but not less than twenty "thousand," shall be substituted for "county "borough":

   (5) References to special county purposes shall not apply:

C

(6) "Burgh general improvement assessment" or any other assessment leviable in equal proportions on owners and occupiers shall be substituted for "borough fund or borough rate"; Provided that any rate under this Act shall not be reckoned in calculating the amount of such assessment for the purpose of any statutory limit on such assessment:

(7) "Inspector" shall include general superintendent and visiting officer:

7 & 58 Vict.
c. 58.

56 & 57 Vict.
c. 73.

(8) Sections forty-seven, fifty-two, and fifty-three of the Local Government (Scotland) Act, 1894, shall be substituted for sections eighty-five, eighty-six, and eighty-eight of the Local Government Act, 1894:

(9) "Municipal elector" shall be substituted for "burgess."

(10) Sub-section three of section two of this Act shall not apply to any county or to any burgh except with the consent of the Local Government Board for Scotland expressed by order made on the application of the county council or town council, as the case may be.

6. In the application of this Act to Ireland— Application to Ireland.

    (1) "The Local Government Board for Ireland" shall be substituted for "the Local Government Board":

See note to Section 5.

    (2) As respects population "ten thousand" shall be substituted for "fifty thousand," and "five thousand," for "ten thousand":

    (3) The provisions of this Act relating to the inclusion of a county borough in a county shall not apply:

    (4) Subsection three of section two of this Act shall not apply to any county in Ireland, except by order of the Local Government Board for Ireland made on the application of the council of that county:

    (5) Articles forty, forty-three, and forty-five of the schedule to the Local Government (Application of Enactments) Order, 1898, shall be substituted for sections eighty-five, eighty-six, and eighty-eight respectively of the Local Government Act, 1894. 56 & 57 Vict. c. 73.

7. This Act may be cited as the Unemployed Workmen Act, 1905. Short title.

Duration of Act.

8. This Act shall continue in force for three years from the date of the passing thereof, and no longer, unless Parliament otherwise determine, and at the expiration of that period, unless this Act is so continued as aforesaid, the Local Government Board shall make such orders as they think necessary for dissolving the central bodies and distress committees established under this Act, and transferring their property and liabilities; and for the purposes of such transfer sections eighty-five, eighty-six, and eighty-eight of the Local Government Act, 1894 (which relate to current rates, existing securities and debts, and pending contracts, &c.), shall apply, with such modifications and adaptations as may be made by order of the Local Government Board.

56 & 57 Vict. c. 73.

Note.—The date of the Act was the 11th August, 1905, the period of the three years, therefore, commenced to run from that date.

The Sections of the Local Government Act, 1894, mentioned in this Section of the Act, are as follows:—

Local Government Act, 1894, 56 and 57 Vict., cap. 73.

Section 85 (1) Every rate and precept for contributions made before the appointed day may be assessed, levied, and collected, and proceedings for the enforcement thereof taken, in like manner as nearly as may be as if this Act had not passed.

(2) The accounts of all receipts and expenditure before the appointed day shall be audited, and disallowances, surcharges, and penalties recovered and enforced, and other consequential proceedings had, in like manner as nearly as may be as if this Act had not passed, but as soon as practicable after the appointed day; and every authority, committee, or officer whose duty it is to make up any accounts, or to account for any portion of the receipts or expenditure in any account shall, until the audit is completed, be deemed for the purpose of such audit to continue in office, and be bound to perform the same duties and render the same accounts and be subject to the same liabilities as before the appointed day.

(3) All proceedings, legal and other, commenced before the appointed day may be carried on in like manner, as nearly as may be as if this Act had not passed, and any such legal proceeding may be amended in such manner as may appear necessary or proper in order to bring it into conformity with the provisions of this Act.

(4) Every valuation list made for a parish divided by this Act shall continue in force until a new valuation list is made.

(5) The change of name of an Urban Sanitary Authority shall not effect their identity as a corporate body or deviate from their powers, and any enactment in any Act, whether public, general, or local and personal, referring to the members of such authority shall, unless inconsistant with this Act, continue to refer to the members of such authority under its new name.

SECTION 86 (1) Nothing in this Act shall prejudicially affect any securities granted before the passing of this Act on the credit of any rate or property transferred to a Council or Parish Meeting by this Act, and all such securities as well as all unsecured debts, liabilities, and obligations incurred by any Authority in the exercise of any powers ; or in relation to any property transferred from them to a Council or Parish Meeting, shall be discharged, paid, and satisfied by that Council or Parish Meeting, and where for that purpose it is necessary to continue the levy of any rate or the exercise of any power which would have existed but for this Act, that rate may continue to be levied and that power to be exercised either by the authority who otherwise would have levied or exercised the same, or by the transferee as the case may require.

(2) It shall be the duty of every authority whose powers, duties, and liabilities are transferred by this Act to liquidate, so far as practicable before the appointed day, all current debts and liabilities incurred by such authority.

SECTION 88 (1) If at the time when any powers, duties, liabilities, debts, or property are by this Act transferred to a Council or parish meeting, any action or proceeding, or any cause of action or proceeding is pending or existing by or against any authority in relation thereto the same shall not be in anywise prejudicially affected by the passing of this Act, but may be continued, prosecuted, and enforced by or against the council or parish meeting as successors of the said authority in like manner as if this Act had not been passed.

Sect. 8.—Note—

(2) All contracts, deeds, bonds, agreements, and other instruments subsisting at the time of the transfer in this section mentioned, and effecting any of such powers, duties, liabilities, debts, or property, shall be of as full force and effect against or in favour of the council or parish meeting, and may be enforced as fully and effectually as if, instead of the authority, the council or parish meeting had been a party thereto.

"THE ORGANISATION (UNEMPLOYED WORKMEN) ESTABLISHMENT ORDER, 1905."

[ORDER FOR LONDON].

———————

To the London County Council:—

To the Mayor, Aldermen, and Commons of the City of London in Common Council assembled;

To the Councils of the several Metropolitan Boroughs;

To the Boards of Guardians of the several Poor Law Unions in the Administrative County of London;

To the several Distress Committees and to the Central Body to be established in pursuance of the Unemployed Workmen Act, 1905, for the said Administrative County;

And to all others whom it may concern.

WHEREAS by sub-sections (1) and (8) of Section 1 of the Unemployed Workmen Act, 1905, it is enacted that:

"**1.** (1) For the purposes of this Act there "shall be established, by Order of the Local "Government Board under this Act, a distress

"committee of the council of every metropolitan
" borough in London, consisting partly of members
" of the borough council and partly of members
" of the board of guardians of every poor law
" union wholly or partly within the borough
" and of persons experienced in the relief of
" distress, and a central body for the whole of the
" administrative county of London, consisting
" partly of members of and selected by the distress
" committees and of members of and selected by
" the London County Council, and partly of
" persons co-opted to be additional members of
" the body, and partly, if the Order so provides,
" of persons nominated by the Local Goverment
" Board, but the number of the persons so co-opted
" and nominated shall not exceed one-fourth of
" the total number of the body, and every such
" order shall provide that one member at least of
" the committee or body established by the order
" shall be a woman.

"(8) This section shall apply to the City of
" London as if the City of London were a metro-
" politan borough, and the mayor, aldermen,
" and commons of the City of London in common
" council assembled were the council of the
" borough, and any contribution required for the
" purposes of this Act shall be paid out of the
" consolidated rate, but shall not be reckoned in
" calculating the amount of the rate for the
" purpose of any limit on that amount."

And whereas by sub-sections (1) and (2) of Section 4 of the Act it is enacted that:—

"4. (1) An order of the Local Government " Board under this Act establishing a central body "or distress committee may provide for the con- "stitution and proceedings of that body or "committee, and, in the case of an order estab- "lishing a central body, for the incorporation of "that body by an appropriate name, and, where "any property or liabilities are taken over from "any other body, for effecting by virtue of the "order the transfer of that property or those "liabilities, and also for any matter for which "provision may be made by regulations under "this Act, and for which it appears desirable to "make special provision affecting only the body "or committee established by the order.

"(2) An order of the Local Government " Board under this Act may be varied and revoked "by any subsequent order of the Board made "under this Act."

NOW THEREFORE, We, the Local Government Board, in the exercise of Our powers in that behalf, do hereby Order as follows, that is to say:—

ARTICLE I. In this Order unless the contrary intention appears:— *Interpretation.*

(*a*) Words importing the masculine gender include females;

Art. I.

(*b*) Words in the singular include the plural, and words in the plural include the singular;

(*c*) The expression "the Act" means the Unemployed Workmen Act, 1905;

The expression "the Common Council," means the Mayor, Aldermen, and Commons of the City of London in Common Council assembled; and

The expression "the County Council" means the London County Council.

Constitution of Distress Committees

ARTICLE II. (1) There shall be established a Distress Committee of the Common Council, and also a Distress Committee of the Council of every Metropolitan Borough.

(2) The Distress Committee of the Common Council shall comprise twenty-five members, that is to say—

Twelve members appointed by the Common Council from their own body;

Eight members appointed by the Common Council and being persons selected by the Board of Guardians of the City of London Union from their own body; and

Five members (of whom one at least shall be a woman) appointed by the Common Council from outside their own body, but from persons experienced in the relief of distress.

Art. II.

(3) The Distress Committee of each Metropolitan Borough Council shall comprise the total number of members specified in relation to the Metropolitan Borough in Column 6 of the Schedule to this Order.

The total number of members specified as aforesaid shall consist of—

(i.) Such number of members appointed by the Borough Council from their own body as is specified in relation to the Metropolitan Borough in Column 3 of the Schedule to this Order;

(ii.) Such number of members appointed by the Borough Council and being persons selected by the Board of Guardians of each Poor Law Union wholly or partly in the Metropolitan Borough as in relation to the Metropolitan Borough and the Poor Law Union named in Column 2 of the Schedule to this Order is specified in Column 4 of that Schedule, opposite to the names of the Metropolitan Borough and Poor Law Union; and

(iii.) Such number of members (of whom one at least shall be a woman) appointed by the Borough Council from outside their own body, but from persons experienced in the relief of distress as is specified in relation to the Metropolitan Borough in Column 5 of the Schedule to this Order.

Art. II.—NOTE—

(1). Constitution of Distress Committee.

This establishment of Distress Committees is in accordance with the requirement of Section 1 (1) of the Act. While Section 1 (1) of the Act names the three constituent parts of each Distress Committee, it is left to the Local Government by Section 4 (1) to prescribe the number of members each part shall have. In their circular letter (20th September, 1905), accompanying the London Order, the Board say that :—

"The Order prescribes the number of members of the Committee. In the case of the City of London, and of each Metropolitan Borough with a population of upwards of 150,000 persons according to the last Census the total number of members is fixed at 25, made up of twelve members appointed by the Council from their own body, eight members appointed by them but selected by the Guardians from their own body, and five persons appointed by the Council from outside their own body but from persons experienced in the relief of distress. In the case of every other Metropolitan Borough the numbers will be ten, six, and four respectively, making a total of twenty members."

"The numbers to be appointed in any particular case will be seen on reference to Article II., and to the Schedule to the Order."

"Where more than one Poor Law Union is wholly or partly within a borough the number of Guardians to be appointed has been divided between the Unions concerned, regard being had to their population and rateable value."

(2). Women Members of Distress Committees.

Section 1 (1) of the Act requires in respect of each Committee that one member at least "shall be a woman." As women are not eligible to be elected Councillors of Metropolitan Boroughs (London Government Act, 1899, Section 2 (1), 62 and 63 Vict., c. 14), and as there is no guarantee of there being any women members of Boards of Guardians, although women are eligible to be elected (Local Government Act, 1894, Section 20 (2), 56 and 57 Vict., c 73), the Board by their Order have met the requirement of the Act by providing that of persons chosen from "persons experienced in the relief of distress" to be members of the Distress Committee, one at least shall be a woman. The Local Government Board observe that "The Council may deem it desirable to appoint more than one woman on the Committee, especially if the representatives of the Guardians do not include a woman." [L.G.B.C.L., 20th September, 1905.]

Art. II.—Note—

(3). Persons experienced in Relief of Distress.

The Unemployed Workmen Bill as originally introduced in the House of Commons, provided for the Distress Committees to be entirely composed of Councillors and Guardians. In Committee the President of the Local Government Board (Mr. G. Balfour, M.P.) proposed an amendment to enlarge the constitution by the addition of "persons of experience in the administration of Charities." After strong objection by Mr. Keir Hardie, M.P., that the words "in the administration of Charities" would lead to the setting up of invidious distinctions under which Secretaries of Trades' Unions and other persons not members of a Charity Organisation Society might be excluded, an amendment in the words "person experienced in the relief of distress," was adopted. A precedent for such co-optation is found in the Elementary Education Act, 1902, Section 17 (3) (*b*) (2 Edward VII., c. 42), where it is made obligatory that "persons of experience in Education" shall be co-opted on the Local Education Committee. There is no stipulation either in the present Act or the Order that the "persons experienced in the relief of distress" shall be either Ratepayers or residents of the area for which the Distress Committee is elected ; nor have the Local Government Board attempted to give any advice in the matter. The selection and the election of such persons from outside the Council to the number specified in Column 5 of the Schedule to the Order, neither more nor less [L.G.B.C.L., 20th September, 1905], is, therefore, a matter entirely for the Council. No one, however, can be elected who is disqualified under Article X of the Order. See Note to that Article.

ARTICLE III (1) At a meeting to be held within three weeks from the date of this Order, or within such further time as We may allow, the Board of Guardians of the City of London Union, and every Board of Guardians of a Poor Law Union wholly or partly in a Metropolitan Borough shall select from their own body the persons who are to be afterwards appointed, in the one case by the Common Council, and, in the other case, by the Borough Council, as members of a Distress Committee; and the Clerk to

Selection and appointment of members of Distress Committees

Art. III.

the Guardians shall forthwith communicate the names, addresses, and descriptions of the said persons to the Common Council or to the Borough Council, as the case may require.

(2) The Common Council and each Borough Council shall, at a meeting to be held before the expiration of five weeks from the date of this Order, or within such further time as We may allow, appoint the members of the Distress Committee of the Common Council or of the Borough Council, as the case may be.

(3) The Town Clerk, or other officer or person by whom notices of meeting of the Common Council or Borough Council are given, shall give to every member not less than seven days' previous notice in writing of the meeting at which the appointment of members of a Distress Committee is to be made and of the intention to make the appointment.

(1) Selection of Guardians as Members of Distress Committee.

The selection is to be made by each Board to whom the Order applies by not later than the 11th October, 1905 [three weeks from the date of the Order], or within such further time as the Local Government Board may allow. "It is desirable that the selection should be made at the earliest possible date and the Board consider it should be made within the three weeks in all cases, unless this is really impracticable". [L.G. B.C.L., 29th September, 1905]. The Order does not require notice to be given to the Guardians of the Meeting at which the selection is to be made. Regulations which the Guardians, as empowered by Sect. 59 (1) of the Local Government Act, 1894, (56 and 57 Vic., c. 73), may have made with respect to notice of meetings and to the transaction and management of their business should however be complied with if time permit. The

Art. III.—Note—

communication to be made by the Clerk to the Guardians of the selection made by the Guardians is to be made forthwith. "Forthwith" has in a number of cases been construed as meaning "within a reasonable time," but it should be taken in the present connexion as meaning "without delay" (per Jessel, M.R., *re* Southan, ex parte Lamb, 51 L.J. ch. 207). The Local Government Board accordingly say that—"As soon as the selection is made, the names, addresses and descriptions of the persons selected are to be sent by the Clerk to the Guardians to the Common Council or the Borough Council, as the case may require."

The communication should be a written notice sent to the Clerk of the Council.

Although the Guardians are only to select, not to appoint, it is the duty of the Council to appoint the Guardians selected not exceeding the number allowed by the Order.

(2) Appointment of the Distress Committee.

The appointment has to be made not later than the 25th October, 1905 (by which date the five weeks from the date of the Order expires) or within such further time as the Local Government Board may allow. "It will probably be convenient that no appointment should be made until each Board of Guardians in the Borough have selected their representatives, as otherwise these representatives must be appointed at a subsequent meeting; but it is desirable that the appointment should take place at the earliest date practicable, and the Board suggest that the Council should ascertain when the names of the persons selected by the Guardians will be received, so that the appointment of the members of the Committee may be made as soon as possible afterwards (L.G.B.C.L., 29th September, 1905).

(3) The Distress Committee a Committee of the Council.

In their Circular Letter of the 29th September, 1905, the Local Government Board, having in mind Section 1 (1) of the Act, point out that the "Distress Committee will be a Committee of the Borough Council." In so far as the actual appointment of the Committee has to be made by the Council, that is so. The Council, however, in appointing the Committee are not left with any discretion as to the size of the Committee, for they must comply with the terms of the Order. Moreover, the procedure of the Committee is prescribed by the Order [Art. XIV] and not left to the Council to prescribe. Therefore:—"Unless Rules [made under Article XIV] so require, it will not be necessary that the acts of the Committee should be submitted for confirmation to the Council by whom they are appointed." [L.G.B.C.L. with Regulations, 10th October, 1905].

Art. III.—Note—

(4) Notice of Council Meeting at which the appointment is to be made.

"Not less than seven days' previous notice" means seven days exclusive of the day on which the notice is given and of the day on which the meeting is held [Zouch *v.* Empsey, 4 B. and Ald. 522; R.v. J. J. Salop, 7 L.J.M.C. 56]. "The giving of this notice need not be deferred until the names of the selected Guardians are received, if it is ascertained at what date they will be received, and the meeting is fixed for some day subsequent to that date. [L.G.B.C.L., 29th September, 1905].

Removal of difficulties in establishment of Committee. See Article XV.

Term of office of members of Distress Committees

ARTICLE IV. (1) A member of a Distress Committee who is a member of the Common Council, of a Borough Council, or of a Board of Guardians shall continue in office until he dies, or resigns, or goes out of office as a member of the Council by whom he was appointed, or of the Board of Guardians by whom he was selected for appointment as a member of a Distress Committee, or until he becomes disqualified by virtue of this Order.

(2) A member of a Distress Committee who has been appointed by the Common Council or by a Borough Council from outside their own body, but from persons experienced in the relief of distress, shall continue in office until he dies, or resigns, or completes the period for which he was appointed to serve as a member of the Distress Committee, or until he becomes disqualified by virtue of this Order:

Provided that a member of a Distress Committee who ceases to hold office in pursuance of this Article shall be re-eligible as a member of the Distress Committee if, at the time of re-appointment, he is qualified to be so re-appointed.

Art. IV.—Note—

(1). Term of Office of Members of Distress Committees.

"Neither the Council nor the Guardians are empowered to deal with this matter as regards their representatives on the Committee, but as regards any member appointed from persons experienced in the relief of distress, it will be competent for the Council to prescribe the period for which he is appointed to serve as a member of the Committee. The Council will probably deem it desirable to exercise this power, and the Board suggest that the first appointment might be made for the period up to the 31st March, 1907, inclusive. If no period is specified, the member will hold office until he dies, or resigns, or becomes disqualified by virtue of the Order" [L.G.B.C.L., 20th September, 1905].

(2). Resignation.

A Councillor or Guardian Member of the Committee, will be at liberty to resign membership of the Committee without resigning his office as a Councillor or Guardian. The Order does not mention as to whom Notice of Resignation is to be given, or when the Resignation is to be considered effected. In the absence of any regulation in the matter it is submitted that a written notice of the resignation, given to the Distress Committee by the member resigning, will be a sufficient resignation, and that the resignation is completely effected on the notice being delivered at a meeting of the Committee or to the clerk of the Committee. If a similar notice be also given to the Council, and in the case of the resignation of a Guardian Member of the Committee to the Board of Guardians, no room will remain for doubt as to the sufficiency of the resignation.

(3). Disqualification for Office. See Article X. of the Order.

ARTICLE V. (1) On a vacancy occurring in a Distress Committee by reason of the death or resignation of a member, or otherwise, the Council by whom that member was appointed shall, subject to this Order, appoint another member in his place.

Casual vacancies in Distress Committees

The person appointed to fill the vacancy shall be appointed at a meeting of the Council to be held within four weeks after the occurrence of that vacancy,

D

Art. V.

or, where the appointment is to be made of a person selected by a Board of Guardians, at that meeting of the Council which will be held immediately after the expiration of seven days from the date of the communication to the Council of the names, address, and description of the person selected, or, in either case, within such farther time as We may allow.

(2) The Town Clerk or other officer or person by whom notices of meeting of the Council are given shall give to each member of the Council seven days' previous notice in writing of the meeting at which the appointment is to be made, and of the intention to make the appointment.

The Town Clerk or other officer or person as aforesaid after any such appointment is made shall forthwith notify in writing to the Clerk to the Distress Committee the names, address, and description of the person appointed.

(1) Notice of Vacancy.

The terms of the Order as to the notice to be given by the Town Clerk, to each member of the Council, of meeting of the Council at which the casual vacancy is to be filled, are identical with the terms *re* original appointment of Committee. See Article III. (5). But the Order contains no directions as to who is to make communication of the fact that a vacancy has arisen. In the case of vacancy by death, resignation or otherwise of a Guardian member of the Committee it is apparently taken for granted :-(1) that the fact of the vacancy will be within the knowledge of the Board of Guardians concerned ; (2) that the Board will proceed as on the occasion of the original selection under Art. III. of the Order, to select a Guardian to fill the vacancies ; and (3) that the communication of the selection will be made, again as on the original Section, by the Clerk to the Guardians [See Art. III. (1)].

Article V—Note—

Where the vacancy arises from the death or going out of office of a Councillor, the fact of course is bound to be within the knowledge of the Council and their Clerk.

The deficiency of the Order in respect of explicit direction as to who is to notify that a casual vacancy has arisen may be met by the Distress Committee giving, in accordance with their powers under Art. XIV. of the Order, such directions to their Clerk as may be deemed necessary. Where vacancy of seat arises from disqualification or absence, the Committee have not only to declare seat vacant, but the vacancy has to be notified in such manner as Committee shall direct. See Local Government Act, 1894 (56 and 57 Vict., c. 73), Section 46 (7), Note to Article X.

(2) Time in which vacancy is to be filled.

Clause (1) of the Article is not very well drawn, but the evident intention is that, where a vacancy occurs in the Distress Committee by the death or resignation of a member, or otherwise, and that member was a Councillor or a member selected from persons experienced in the relief of distress, the vacancy shall be filled within four weeks after the occurrence of the vacancy, but if the member was a Guardian then the vacancy shall be filled at the Council meeting held as soon as may be (for that is the meaning of the word "immediately" as used in the Art.) after communication made by the Clerk to the Guardians of the person selected by the Guardians to fill the vacancy, and the Town Clerk has given the requisite notice required by Clause (2) of the Article. There is no stated time in which the Guardians are to select one of their number to fill vacancy.

(3) Meaning of Terms.

"Within four weeks after the occurrence." The first day of the four weeks is the day that next follows the day of the occurrence. On the expression "Forthwith" see Note (1) on Art. III., and on expression "Seven days" see Note (4) on Art. III.

ARTICLE VI. (1) There shall be established a Central Body for the Administrative County of London.

The Central Body shall be a body corporate by the name of "The Central (Unemployed) Body for London," with perpetual succession, and a common seal,

Art. VI.

and with power to sue and be sued in that name, and to
hold lands without any licence in mortmain for the
purposes of the Act.

(2) The Central Body shall comprise—

Four members selected from their own body by
the County Council;

Four members selected in each case from their
own body by the Distress Committee of the
Common Council and by the Distress Committee
of the Council of the Metropolitan Borough of
Westminster;

Two members selected in each case from their
own body by the Distress Committee of every
other Borough Council;

Such number of members (not exceeding eight)
as may be nominated by Us; and

Eight persons (of whom one at least shall be a
woman) co-opted to be additional members of the
Central Body by the members selected and
nominated as aforesaid.

(1). Constitution of Central Body.

This Establishment of Central Body is in accordance with
requirement of Section 4 (1) of the Act. While Section 4 (1) of
the Act names the four (three obligatory and one at the option
of the Local Government Board) constituent parts of Central
Body, it is left to the Board by Section 4 (1) to prescribe
the proportionate parts subject to the limitation made by

ART. VI.—NOTE—

Section 1 (1) as to the number of persons co-opted by the Central Body and the persons nominated by the said Board. The total membership of the Central Body as provided for in the Order is 84. The number of nominated and co-opted members provided for is 16, or rather less than one-fifth of the total. The one-fifth proportion is the proportion adopted for the Distress Committees in respect of the person elected on those Committees from "persons experienced in the relief of distress."

(2). The Central Body a Body Corporate.

The provision of the order making the Central Body a Body Corporate with perpetual succession, &c., is in accordance with the delegated legislative authority given to the Local Government Board by Section 4 of the Act. The Central Body will therefore have the status of Local Authorities under the Local Government Acts.

(3). Perpetual Succession and Common Seal.

The Act is only for three years and, if there should be no renewal or extension of, or substitution for, its provisions, the Central Body must cease to exist. The expression "Perpetual Succession" in the order means that the succession of the Central Body as a corporation is preserved and unaffected notwithstanding any changes there may be by individuals going out of, or coming into membership. The Common Seal is the symbol of Incorporation and is in the making of contracts, &c., the corporation's "hand and mouthpiece."

(4). Lands.

The explanation of the right given "to hold lands without license in mortmain for the purposes of the Act," is that in Section 1 (1) of the Mortmain and Charitable Uses Act, 1888 (51 and 52 Vict. C. 42), it is enacted that land shall not be assured to or for the benefit of, or acquired by or on behalf of any Corporation in mortmain, otherwise than under the authority of a license from the Crown, or of a Statute for the time being in force, and that if any land is so assured otherwise than as aforesaid the land shall be forfeited to the Crown.

The said Act of 1888, is an Act amending and consolidating the old Statutes prohibiting under pain of forfeiture the alienation of land "to religious and other corporations which were supposed to hold them in a dead or unserviceable hand."

Art. VI.—Note—

Land is defined by Section 3 of The Mortmain and Charitable Uses Act, 1891, (54 and 55 Vict. C. 73) as including tenements and hereditaments corporeal or incorporeal of any tenure, but not money secured, or land, or other personal estate arising from or connected with land.

(5). Nominated and Co-opted Members.

The Unemployed Workmens Bill, as originally introduced in the House of Commons, provided for the Central Body to be constituted of members of the Distress Committees and of the London County Council, with power to co-opt additional members up to a fourth of the total number of the body. There was no provision for the Local Government Board to nominate members. This provision was added during the Committee stage in the House of Commons on an amendment (at once adopted by the House) of Captain Jessel, M.P. for St. Pancras, who pointed out that such a provision would enable the Board to bring into the Central Body well-known men, such as Mr. Charles Booth, the Bishop of Stepney, and Mr. Steadman, who otherwise might not find a seat on this body. A precedent for vesting such power in the Local Government Board is contained in Section 11 of the Metropolitan Poor Act, 1867 (30 Vict. C. 6) under which the said Board nominate members of the Metropolitan Asylums Board. It will be found on reference to Section 1 (1) of the present Act, that it is not insisted upon by the terms of the Act, that there shall be nominated members on "the Central (Unemployed) Body for London." There are only to be such members if the Local Government Board's Order so provides. The present Order so provides.

The nomination completes the Election.

No qualification is laid down in the Act or Order with respect to either nominated or co-opted members. They need not be resident in London, nor Ratepayers. They must, however, be persons who are not disqualified by Article X.—See that Article and the note thereon.

(6). Women Members of the Central Body.

Section 1 (1) of the Act requires that at least one member of the Central Body "shall be a woman." This requirement is met by the Order providing that of the eight co-opted members "one at least shall be a woman."

See further Note (2) to Article II.

ARTICLE VII. (1) The County Council at a meeting to be held within six weeks from the date of this Order, and each Distress Committee at a meeting to be held within two weeks after their appointment, or within such further time as We may allow, shall select such number of members of the Central Body as the Council or the Distress Committee are entitled to select.

Appointment, &c., of members of Central Body.

(2) The Clerk, or other officer or person by whom notices of meeting of the Council or Distress Committee are given, shall give to each member not less than seven days' previous notice in writing of the meeting at which members of the Central Body are to be selected and of the intention to make the selection.

The Clerk or other officer or person aforesaid, after the selection of members, shall forthwith cause the names, addresses, and descriptions of the several members selected to be transmitted to Us.

(3) After the selection of members of the Central Body by the Council and by the several Distress Committees, and the nomination of members by Us, the members of the Central Body shall, for the purpose of co-opting additional members, attend a preliminary meeting at a time and place to be fixed by Us and in other respects in accordance with arrangements to be made by Us.

Art. VII.

Every member who desires to propose that the Central Body shall co-opt a person as an additional member shall, not less than seven days before the date appointed by Us for the preliminary meeting, transmit the names, address, and description of the person to Us.

(4) The first meeting of the Central Body shall be held at a time and place to be fixed by Us.

(1). Appointment of the Members of Central Body.

The period of six weeks from the date of the Order (20th September, 1905) expires on the 1st November, 1905, by that date therefore the County Council must appoint their members on the Central Body, unless the Local Government Board extend the time. Any Distress Committee not appointed until the 25th October, 1905 (see Article III.), will have until the 8th November for the appointment of their members on the Central Body, but if appointed before the 25th October, then their appointment of their members on the Central Body will be so much earlier than the 8th November, as the fourteen days from the day of the Committee itself being appointed will make it. "It is desirable that the selection should be made within the precise periods mentioned in the Article, so that the Central Body may be constituted as soon as possible."—[L.G.B.C.L., 20th September, 1905.]

(2) Notice of Council or Distress Committee Meeting to appoint Representatives.

See Note (4) to Article III.

(3). Notice of desire to propose to co-opt a person.

Care should be taken (1) that notice by letter, addressed to the Secretary of the Board, is sent by the time required, and (2) that it contains the information required by the Article, viz.: the full name, address, and the trade, profession or rank of the person to be proposed. The Central Body will have to make its own regulations as to any notice required for proposal to co-opt on vacancy occurring, or on term of service expiring.

(4). Meaning of Terms.

For the reckoning of time, and explanation of the expression "forthwith," see Note (4) and Note (1) to Article III.

ARTICLE VIII. A member of the Central Body who has been selected by the County Council, or by a Distress Committee, shall continue in office until he dies or resigns or goes out of office as a member of the Council or Distress Committee or until he becomes disqualified by virtue of this Order.

An additional member of the Central Body shall continue in office until he dies or resigns or completes the period for which he was co-opted or until he becomes disqualified by virtue of this Order.

A member nominated by Us shall continue in office until he dies or resigns or completes the period for which he was nominated, or until his nomination is cancelled, or until he becomes disqualified by virtue of this Order:

Provided that a selected member, or an additional member of the Central Body, who ceases to hold office in pursuance of this Article shall be re-eligible as a member of the Central Body if at the time of his being again selected or co-opted he is qualified to be so selected or co-opted.

(1) Term of Office of Members of Central Body.

The term of office is conditioned in the same way as the term of office of members of the Distress Committee under Article IV., save as to nominated members.

(2) Resignation.

A member of the Central Body who is a Distress Committee representative will be able to resign his or her membership of the Central Body without resigning membership of the Distress Committee.

Term office of members of Central Body.

Art. VIII.—NOTE—

As to Order making no mention as to whom Notice of Resignation is to be sent or when Resignation is to be considered effected, see Note (2) Article IV.

In the absence of any regulation in the matter it is submitted that Resignation should be by notice delivered at a meeting of the Central Body or to the Clerk of that Body.

Casual vacancies in Central Body.

ARTICLE IX. On a vacancy occurring in the Central Body by reason of the death or resignation of a member or otherwise, the Council or Distress Committee by whom that member was selected, or, in the case of an additional member, the Central Body shall, subject to this Order, select or co-opt another member in his place.

The person selected or co-opted to fill the vacancy shall be selected at a meeting of the Council or Distress Committee, or co-opted at a meeting of the Central Body, to be held within four weeks after the occurrence of the vacancy or within such further time as We may allow.

The Clerk or other officer or person by whom notices of meeting of the Council, Distress Committee, or Central Body are given shall give seven days' previous notice in writing of the meeting at which the selection is to be made or the additional member is to be co-opted.

The Clerk or other person as aforesaid shall, after any such selection by the Council or a Distress Committee, forthwith notify in writing to the Clerk to the Central Body the names, address, and occupation of the person selected.

ART. IX.—NOTE—

(1) Notice of Vacancy.

The Order contains no direction as to who shall notify the County Council or the Distress Committee that a vacancy has occurred in their representation on the Central Body—a similar deficiency exists under Article V., see Note (1) Art. V. as to how deficiency may be met, substituting in that note Central Body for Distress Committee.

The terms of the Article as to notice to be given by Town Clerk or Committee Clerk of meeting of Council or Committee to fill vacancy are not identical with the terms *re* original appointment (see Article VII. (2)). No doubt the intention is the same and should be observed as such.

(2) Time in which to fill vacancy, &c.

For reckoning of "Time" and expression "Forthwith" see Note (1) and Note (1) to Art. III.

ARTICLE X. Section 46 of the Local Government Act, 1894, shall apply to a Distress Committee, and to the Central Body, and to any member, as if, with the necessary modifications, the said section were herein re-enacted and in terms made applicable; and every person disqualified by the said section as so applied shall become disqualified by virtue of this Order.

Disqualifications.

NOTE.—The Section mentioned in this Article is as follows:—

Local Government Act 1894 [56 and 57 Vict., c. 73], Section 46 (1). A person shall be disqualified for being elected or being a member or chairman of a council of a parish or of a district other than a borough or of a board of guardians if he

    (a) is an infant or an alien; or

    (b) has within twelve months before his election, or since his election, received union or parochial relief; or

    (c) has, within five years before his election or since his election, been convicted either on indictment or summarily of any crime, and sentenced to imprisonment with hard labour without the option of a fine, or to any greater punishment, and has not received a free pardon, or has, within or during the time aforesaid, been adjudged bankrupt, or made a composition or arrangement with his creditors; or (*d*) holds any paid office under the parish council or district council or board of guardians, as the case may be; or

(*e*) is concerned in any bargain or contract entered into with the council or board, or participates in the profit of any such bargain or contract or of any work done under the authority of the council or board.

(2). Provided that a person shall not be disqualified for being elected or being a member or chairman of any such council or board by reason of being interested—

(*a*) in the sale or lease of any lands or in any loan of money to the council or board, or in any contract with the council for the supply from land, of which he is owner or occupier, of stone, gravel, or other materials for making or repairing highways or bridges, or in the transport of materials for the repair of roads or bridges in his own immediate neighbourhood; or

(*b*) in any newspaper in which any advertisement relating to the affairs of the council or board is inserted; or

(*c*) in any contract with the council or board as a shareholder in any joint stock company; but he shall not vote at any meeting of the council or board on any question in which such company are interested, excepted that in the case of a water company or other company established for the carrying on of works of a like public nature, this prohibition may be dispensed with by the county council.

(3). Where a person who is a parish councillor, or is a candidate for election as a parish councillor, is concerned in any such bargain or contract, or participates in any such profit, as would disqualify him for being a parish councillor, the disqualification may be removed by the county council if they are of opinion that such removal will be beneficial to the parish.

(4). Where a person is disqualified by being adjudged bankrupt or making a composition or arrangement with his creditors, the disqualification shall cease, in case of bankruptcy, when the adjudication is annulled, or when he obtains his discharge with a certificate that his bankruptcy was caused by misfortune without any misconduct on his part, and, in case of composition or arrangement, on payment of his debts in full.

Art. X.—Note—

(5). A person disqualified for being a guardian shall also be disqualified for being a rural district councillor.

(6). If a member of a council of a parish, or of a district other than a borough, or of a board of guardians, is absent from meetings of the council or board for more than six months consecutively, except in case of illness, or for some reason approved by the council or board, his office shall on the expiration of those months become vacant.

(7). Where a member of a council or a board of guardians becomes disqualified for holding office, or vacates his seat for absence, the council or board shall forthwith declare the office to be vacant, and signify the same by notice signed by three members and countersigned by the clerk of the council or board, and notified in such manner as the council or board direct, and the office shall thereupon become vacant.

(8). If any person acts when disqualified, or votes when prohibited under this section, he shall for each offence be liable on summary conviction to a fine not exceeding twenty pounds.

(9). This section shall apply in the case of any authority whose members are elected in accordance with this Act in like manner as if that authority were a district council, and in the case of London auditors as if they were members of a district council.

In the foregoing Section the following modifications should be observed :—

(1). "Distress Committee" or "Central Body" should be substituted for such expressions as "Council of a Parish" or "of a District other than a Borough" or "Board of Guardians" or "Parish Council" or "District Council" or "Council or Board" as the case may require.

(2). "Members of a Distress Committee or Central Body" should be substituted for "Parish Councillor."

(3). Sub-Section (5) should be read as deleted.

On the provisions of the above Section it may be further stated as follows :—

(a). *Infancy.*

Full age is attained on the day before the 21st birthday.

(b). *Alien.*

On any question as to who may be an Alien, the Naturalization Act, 1870 (33 and 34 Vict., C. 14), should be referred to.

Art. X.—Note—

(c). Relief.

See Index under "Relief."

(d). Crime.

A conviction on an offence punishable with imprisonment on summary conviction is a crime that disqualifies. Conybeare v. London School Board, 60 L.J., Q.B. 44 : 63 L.T. (N.S.) 651 : 55 J.P. 151.

(e). Bankruptcy.

In R. v. Cooban (56 L.J.M.C. 33 : 51 J.P. 500) it was held that under Rule 5 of Schedule II. to Public Health Act, 1875 (38 and 39 Vict. C. 55), an assignment of property for benefit of creditors was not necessarily a composition with creditors disqualifying for membership of a Local Board. Section 46 (1) (c) of the Local Government Act, 1894 (56 and 57 Vict. C. 73), it will be noticed, makes "an arrangement with creditors," which the said Rule did not, a disqualification, and therefore such an assignment of property as mentioned is apparently an arrangement that disqualifies.

(f) Disqualification for absence.

It is advisable that before a seat is declared vacant for absence the member should be afforded an opportunity to explain his absence (Richardson v. Metley School Board 62 L.J. Ch. 945 : 69 L.T. (N.S.) 308).

(g). Declaration of Vacancy.

The office is not actually vacant until the requirements of of Sub-Section (7) as to declaration has been complied with. R. v. Mayor, &c., of Leeds, 7 A. and E. 963 : Hardwicke v. Brown, 28 L.T (N.S.) 502 : 37 J.P. 407 ; R. v. Mayor, &c., of Welshpool, 35 L.T. (N.S.) 598.

First meeting of Distress Committee]

ARTICLE XI. The time and place of holding the first meeting of the Distress Committee of the Common Council and of the Distress Committee of the Council of every Metropolitan Borough shall be fixed by the Common Council in the one case and by the Borough Council in every other case.

Convener and Notice of Meeting.

As the Order makes no provision as to who shall be convener of the first meeting of the Distress Committee, it will be necessary for the Council to appoint a convener. The first meeting should "be held as soon as possible after the appointment of the Committee." [L.G.B.C.L., 20th September, 1905.]

Art. XI.—Note:—

As the Committee have at their first meeting to appoint a Chairman [Article XII.], and have, within fourteen days of their appointment, to appoint representatives on the Central Body [Article VII (1)] the notice convening the meeting should state that among the items of business to be transacted at the meeting will be the appointment of a Chairman and of the representatives mentioned. A Vice-Chairman is mentioned in Article XIV., but he need not be appointed at the first meeting.

ARTICLE XII. Each Distress Committee and the Central Body at their first meeting, and thereafter as occasion requires, shall appoint one of their number to be Chairman.

Chairman of Distress Committee and Central Body.

The term of office of the Chairman shall be such as the Distress Committee or the Central Body appoint, but if during that term the Chairman of the Distress Committee ceases to be a member of the Council by whom he was appointed, or of the Board of Guardians by whom he was selected for appointment as a member of the Distress Committee, or ceases to be a Member of the Distress Committee from any other cause, or the Chairman of the Central Body ceases to be a member of the Council or Distress Committee by whom he was selected to be a member of the Central Body, or ceases to be a nominated member or to be co-opted as an additional member of the Central Body, the Distress Committee or the Central Body, as the case may be, shall forthwith proceed to appoint another person to be Chairman for the rest of the term.

NOTE.—As to appointment of a Vice-Chairman see Article XIV., an for expression " forthwith " see Note (1) to Article III.

Meetings.

ARTICLE XIII. After the first meeting, all ordinary meetings of a Distress Committee or of the Central Body shall be held at such times and places as are appointed by the Distress Committee or the Central Body.

An extraordinary meeting of a Distress Committee or of the Central Body shall be summoned by the Chairman on his own responsibility or on the receipt of a requisition in writing from any three members of the Distress Committee or of the Central Body, but no business other than that specified in the summons for the extraordinary meeting shall be transacted at that meeting.

NOTE.—See under Act XIV.

Procedure.

ARTICLE XIV. Every question at a meeting of a Distress Committee or of the Central Body shall be decided by a majority of votes of the members present and voting on that question, and in the case of equality of votes the person presiding at the meeting shall have a second or casting vote.

The quorum of a Distress Committee or of the Central Body shall be one-third of the whole number of members of the Distress Committee, or of the Central Body.

A Distress Committee or the Central Body may appoint from among their members such and so many Committees, either of a general or special nature, and consisting of such number of persons as the Distress

Art. XIV.

Committee or the Central Body think fit for any purposes which, in their opinion, would be better regulated and managed by means of Committees, and may delegate with or without any restrictions or conditions any of their powers and duties; and the quorum, proceedings, and place of meeting of any Committee shall be such as may be determined by regulations of the body appointing the Committee.

Subject to the provisions of the Act and of any Regulations under the Act, a Distress Committee and the Central Body may regulate their own procedure and may make rules with respect to the appointment and duties of a Vice-Chairman and generally with respect to the transaction and management of their business.

Meetings and Procedure.

As to removal of any difficulty arising with respect to first meeting see Article XV.

The provisions of the Order in these respects appear to have been framed on certain provisions in the Municipal Corporations Act, 1882 [45 and 46 Vict. c. 50] Section 22 and second Schedule. In making rules under Article XIV. as regards the calling of meetings, the following rules in the said Schedule may be found suggestive.

"Rule 3. The Mayor may at any time call a meeting of the Council."

"Rule 4. If the Mayor refuses to call a meeting after a requisition for that purpose, signed by five members of the Council, has been presented to him, any five members of the Council may forthwith on that refusal call a meeting. If the Mayor (without so refusing) does not within seven days after such presentation call a meeting any five members of the Council may, on the expiration of those seven days, call a meeting."

E

Art. XIV.—Note.—

"Rule 6   Three clear days at least before any meeting of the Council, a summons to attend the meeting, specifying the business proposed to be transacted thereat and signed by the Town Clerk, shall be left or delivered by post in a registered letter at the usual place of abode of every member of the Council three clear days at least before the meeting."

"Rule 7.   Want of service of the summons on any member of the Council shall not affect the validity of a meeting."

"Rule 8.   No business shall be transacted at a meeting other than that specified in the summons relating thereto, except, in case of a quarterly meeting, business prescribed by this Act to be transacted thereat."

Removal of difficulties.

ARTICLE XV.   If any difference or difficulty arises with respect to the establishment of a Distress Committee or of the Central Body, or with respect to the appointment of members of a Distress Committee or with respect to the selection of members of the Central Body or with respect to the number of members of a Distress Committee whom a Council may be entitled to appoint after selection by a Board of Guardians, or with respect to the first meeting of a Distress Committee or of the Central Body, We may by Order do anything which appears to Us to be necessary or expedient for the determination of any such difference or the removal of any such difficulty or for the proper establishment of a Distress Committee or of the Central Body, or for the proper holding of the first meeting of a Distress Committee or of the Central Body.

Short title.

ARTICLE XVI.   This Order may be cited as "The Organisation (Unemployed Workmen) Establishment Order, 1905."

SCHEDULE.

Constitution of Distress Committees.

		Number of Members appointed			
Metropolitan Borough.	Poor Law Union wholly or partly in the Metropolitan Borough.	From Council	From Guardians.	From Persons experienced in Relief of Distress.	Total Number.
Battersea ...	... Wandsworth ...	12	8	5	25
Bermondsey ...	... Bermondsey ...	10	6	4	20
Bethnal Green ...	... Saint Matthew, Bethnal Green.	10	6	4	20
Camberwell ...	... Saint Giles, Camberwell.	12	8	5	25
Chelsea ...	... Saint Luke, Chelsea.	10	6	4	20
Deptford ...	... Greenwich ...	10	6	4	20
Finsbury ...	... Holborn ...	10	6	4	20
Fulham ...	... Fulham ...	10	6	4	20
Greenwich	{ Greenwich ...	—	4	—	—
	{ Woolwich ...	—	2	—	—
		10	6	4	20
Hackney ...	... Hackney ...	12	8	5	25
Hammersmith ...	... Hammersmith ...	10	6	4	20
Hampstead ...	... Saint John Hampstead.	10	6	4	20
Holborn ...	{ Saint Giles-in-the-Fields and Saint George, Bloomsbury.	—	3	—	—
	{ Holborn ...	—	3	—	—
		10	6	4	20

Metropolitan Borough	Poor Law Union wholly or partly in the Metropolitan Borough	Number of Members appointed.			
		From Council	From Guardians	From Persons experienced in Relief of Distress	Total Number
Islington ...	... Saint Mary, Islington.	12	8	5	25
Kensington	{ Saint Mary Abbots Kensington.	12	8	5	25
Lambeth ...	... Lambeth ...	12	8	5	25
Lewisham ...	... Lewisham ...	10	6	4	20
Paddington	... Paddington ...	10	6	4	20
Poplar ...	... Poplar ...	12	8	5	25
Saint Marylebone ..	Saint Marylebone.	10	6	4	20
Saint Pancras	... Saint Pancras	12	8	5	25
Shoreditch	... Saint Leonard, Shoreditch.	10	6	4	20
Southwark	... Southwark ...	12	8	5	25
Stepney ...	{ Mile End Old Town.	—	2	—	—
	{ Saint George in the East.	—	2	—	—
	{ Stepney ...	—	2	—	—
	{ Whitechapel ...	—	2	—	—
		12	8	5	25
Stoke Newington...	Hackney ...	10	6	4	20
Wandsworth	... Wandsworth ...	12	8	5	25
Westminster	{ Saint George's...	—	4	—	—
	{ Strand ...	—	2	—	—
	{ Westminster ...	—	2	—	—
		12	8	5	25
Woolwich ...	{ Lewisham ...	—	1	—	—
	{ Woolwich ...	—	5	—	—
		10	6	4	20

Given under the Seal of Office of the Local Government Board, this Twentieth day of September, in the year One thousand nine hundred and five.

G. W. BALFOUR,

President.

L. S.

S. B. PROVIS,
    Secretary.

"THE URBAN DISTRESS COMMITTEES (UNEMPLOYED WORKMEN) ESTABLISHMENT ORDER, 1905."

(Order for Provincial Boroughs and Urban Districts
with a population of not less than 50,000
at last census).

To the Council of every MUNICIPAL BOROUGH
and URBAN DISTRICT in ENGLAND and WALES
to which this Order applies ;—

[NOTE.—See Schedule].

To the Board of Guardians of every Poor Law
Union wholly or partly comprised in any
such Municipal Borough or Urban District ;—

To every Distress Committee to be established in
pursuance of this Order ;—

And to all others whom it may concern.

WHEREAS by Section 2 (1) of the Unemployed
Workmen Act, 1905, it is enacted that :—

" **2.** (1) There shall be established by order
" of the Local Government Board for each muni-
" cipal borough and urban district with a popula-

" tion according to the last census for the time
" being of not less than fifty thousand, and not
" being a borough or district to which the pro-
" visions of section one of this Act have been
" extended, a distress committee of the council
" for the purposes of this Act, with a similar
" constitution to that of a distress committee in
" London, and the distress committee so estab-
" lished shall, as regards their borough or district,
" have the same duties and powers, so far as
" applicable, as are given by this Act to the
" distress committees and central body in
" London."

And whereas the effect of Section 1 (1) of the said
Act, in relation to the constitution of a Distress
Committee of the Council of every Metropolitan
Borough in London, is that the Distress Committee
shall consist partly of members of the Borough Council
and partly of members of every Board of Guardians in
the Borough, and of persons experienced in the relief
of distress, and that every Order establishing a Distress
Committee shall provide that one member at least shall
be a woman ;

And whereas by sub-sections (1) and (2) of Section
4 of the Act it is enacted that : —

" **4.** (1) An order of the Local Government
" Board under this Act establishing a central
" body or distress committee may provide for the

"constitution and proceedings of that body or
"committee, and, in the case of an order estab-
"lishing a central body, for the incorporation of
"that body by an appropriate name, and, where
"any property or liabilities are taken over from
"any other body, for effecting by virtue of the
"order the transfer of that property or those
"liabilities, and also for any matter for which
"provision may be made by regulations under
"this Act, and for which it appears desirable to
"make special provision affecting only the body
"or committee established by the order.

"(2) An order of the Local Government
"Board under this Act may be varied, and
"revoked, by any subsequent order of the Board
"made under this Act."

NOW THEREFORE, We, the Local Government
Board, in the exercise of Our powers in that behalf, do
hereby Order as follows: that is to say—

Interpre-
tation.

ARTICLE I.   In this Order, unless the contrary
intention appears:—

    (*a*) Words importing the masculine gender include
        females;

    (*b*) Words in the singular include the plural, and
        words in the plural include the singular;

Article I.

      (c) The expression "the Act" means the Unemployed Workmen Act, 1905; and the expressions "Borough" and "Urban District" mean and include each Municipal Borough and each Urban District with a population according to the last census for the time being, of not less than fifty thousand, and not being a Borough or District to which the provisions of Section One of the Act have been extended.

    NOTE.—The present Order applies to all Outside London Urban Districts (including Boroughs) in England and Wales, of a population of not less than 50,000 at the census of 1901, named in the Schedule to the Order.

    See Section 1 (9) of the Act for dealing with any Borough or District adjoining or near to London, as if it were within the Administrative County of London.

ARTICLE II. (1) There shall be established a Distress Committee of the Council of each Borough, and of the Council of each Urban District.

    (2) The Distress Committee shall comprise the total number of members specified in relation to the Borough or Urban District in Column 6 of the Schedule to this Order.

    The total number of members specified as aforesaid shall consist of —

      (i.) Such number of members appointed by the Council from their own body as in relation to the Borough or Urban District named in

Constitution of Distress Committee.

Article 11.

Column 1 of the Schedule to this Order is specified in Column 3 of that Schedule opposite to the name of the Borough or Urban District;

(ii.) Such number of members appointed by the Council and being persons selected by the Board of Guardians of each Poor Law Union wholly or partly in the Borough or Urban District as in relation to the Borough or Urban District and the Poor Law Union named in Columns 1 and 2 of the Schedule to this Order is specified in Column 4 of that Schedule, opposite to the names of the Borough or Urban District and Poor Law Union; and

(iii.) Such number of members (of whom one at least shall be a woman) appointed by the Council from outside their own body, but from persons experienced in the relief of distress as is specified in relation to the Borough or Urban District in Column 5 of the Schedule to this Order.

(1). Constitution of Distress Committee.

This establishment of Distress Committees is in accordance with the requirement of Section 2 (1) of the Act. Section 1 (1) names the three constituent parts of each Distress Committee, but it is left to the Local Government Board by Section 4 (1) to prescribe the number of members each part shall have. In their circular letter of the 20th September, 1905, accompanying the present (Outside London) Order, the Board say that :—

Article II.—Note:—

"The Order prescribes the number of members of the Distress Committee. In the case of boroughs with a population of upwards of 400,000 persons according to the last census, the total number of members is fixed at 40, made up of 18 members appointed by the council from their own body, 14 members appointed by them but selected by the guardians from their own body, and 8 persons appointed by the council from outside their own body but from persons experienced in the relief of distress. In the case of boroughs with a population between 200,000 and 400,000 the numbers will be 16, 12, and 7 respectively, making a total of 35 members, whilst in the case of boroughs and urban districts with a population between 100,000 and 200,000 the numbers will be 14, 10, and 6 respectively, making a total of 30 members. In the case of any other borough or urban district the numbers will be 12, 8, and 5 respectively, making a total of 25 members.

"The numbers to be appointed in any particular case will be seen on reference to Article II. and to the Schedule to the Order.

"Where more than one poor law union is wholly or partly within a borough the number of guardians to be appointed has been divided between the unions concerned, regard being had to their population and rateable value."

(2). Women Members of Distress Committees.

Women are not eligible for election as Borough Councillors [Beresford Hope v. Lady Sandhurst, 58 L.J.Q.B. 316; 61 L.T. (N.S.) 150; 53 J.P. 805], but are eligible to be elected Councillors for an Urban District not a Borough [Local Government Act, 1894, 56 and 57 Vict. C. 73. Section 23 (2)], and as Guardians [said Act, Section 20 (2)]. Why women are eligible for election to Distress Committee see Note (2) to Article II. of the London Order.

(3). Persons experienced in Relief of Distress.

See Note (3) to Article II. of the London Order and read Note as if inserted here.

ARTICLE III. (1) At a meeting to be held within three weeks from the date of this Order, or within such further time as We may allow, every Board of Guardians of a Poor Law Union wholly or partly in

Selection and appointment of members of Distress Committees

the Borough or Urban District, shall select from their
own body the persons who are to be afterwards
appointed by the Council as members of the Distress
Committee, and the Clerk to the Guardians shall forthwith communicate to the Council the names, addresses,
and descriptions of the said persons.

(2) The Council shall appoint the members of the
Distress Committee at a meeting to be held before the
expiration of five weeks from the date of this Order, or
within such further time as We may allow.

(3) The Town Clerk or Clerk shall give to every
member of the Council not less than seven days'
previous notice in writing of the meeting at which the
appointment of members of the Distress Committee
is to be made and of the intention to make the
appointment.

(1). Selection of Guardians as Members of Distress Committee.

See Note (1) of the Article III. of the London Order and
read Note as if inserted here, substituting for the expression
"Common Council or Borough Council" the expression
"Borough or Urban District Council."

(2). Appointment of the Distress Committee.

See Note (2) to Article III. of the London Order and
read Note as if inserted here, adding after the word "Borough"
in the L.G.B.C.L., 20th September, 1905, quoted in the Note
the words "or Urban District."

(3). The Distress Committee a Committee of the Council.

In the Circular accompanying the Order the Local
Government Board point out that the "Distress Committee
will be a Committee of the Borough or Urban District
Council." In as far as the Council have to appoint the
Committee that is so. The Act requires it to be so [Section 1
(1) and Section 2 (1), but the Council are left with no discretion
as to the size of the Committee. They must comply with the

Article III.—Note.—

terms of the Order. Moreover the procedure of the Committee is prescribed by the Order [Article X] and not left to the Council to prescribe. Therefore:—"Unless the Rules (made under Article X.) so require, it will not be necessary that the Acts of the Committee should be submitted for confirmation to the Council by whom they are appointed." (L.G.B.C.L., with Regulations 10th October, 1905).

(4). Notice of Council Meeting at which appointment is to be made.

See Note (4) to Article III of the London Order and read Note as if inserted here.

(5). Removal of difficulties in establishment of Committee, &c.
See Article XI.

ARTICLE IV. (1) A member of the Distress Committee who is a member of the Council, or of a Board of Guardians, shall continue in office until he dies, or resigns, or goes out of office as a member of the Council by whom he was appointed, or of the Board of Guardians by whom he was selected for appointment as a member of the Distress Committee, or until he becomes disqualified by virtue of this Order.

(2) A member of the Distress Committee who has been appointed by the Council from outside their own body, but from persons experienced in the relief of distress, shall continue in office until he dies or resigns, or completes the period for which he was appointed to serve as a member of the Distress Committee, or until he becomes disqualified by virtue of this Order:

Provided that a member of the Distress Committee who ceases to hold office in pursuance of this Article, shall be re-eligible as a member of the Distress Committee if, at the time of re-appointment, he is qualified to be so re-appointed.

[Margin: Term of office of members of Distress Committee.]

Article IV.- Note—

(1). Term of Office of Members of Distress Committees.

See opinion of Local Government Board quoted in Note (1) to Article IV. of the London Order.

(2). Resignation.

See Note (2) to Article IV. of the London Order and read Note as if inserted here.

(3). Disqualification for Office.

See Article VI.

Casual vacancies in Distress Committees

ARTICLE V. (1) On a vacancy occurring in the Distress Committee by reason of the death or resignation of a member, or otherwise, the Council by whom that member was appointed shall, subject to this Order, appoint another member in his place.

The person appointed to fill the vacancy shall be appointed at a meeting of the Council to be held within four weeks after the occurrence of that vacancy, or where the appointment is to be made of a person selected by a Board of Guardians at that meeting of the Council which will be held immediately after the expiration of seven days from the date of the communication to the Council of the names, address, and description of the person selected, or in either case within such further time as We may allow.

(2) The Town Clerk, or Clerk, shall give to each member of the Council seven days' previous notice in writing of the meeting at which the appointment is to be made, and of the intention to make the appointment.

Article V.

The Town Clerk, or Clerk, after any such appointment is made, shall forthwith notify in writing to the Clerk to the Distress Committee, the names, address, and description of the person appointed.

(1) Notice of Vacancy.

(2) Time in which Vacancy is to be filled.

(3) Meaning of Terms.

On these three points see Notes (1), (2) and (3), respectively, to Article V. of the London Order and read such Notes as if here inserted, with the following emendations, viz:—In Note (1) for Article XIV., read Article X., and in Note (2) after "Town Clerk" read "or Clerk."

ARTICLE VI. Section 46 of the Local Government Act, 1894, shall apply to a Distress Committee and to any member as if, with the necessary modifications, the said section were herein re-enacted, and in terms made applicable: and every person disqualified by the said section as so applied shall become disqualified by virtue of this Order. Disqualifications.

NOTE.—See Notes to Article X. of the London Order and read as if inserted here.

ARTICLE VII. The time and place of holding the first meeting of a Distress Committee shall be fixed by the Council. First meeting of Distress Committee.

Convener and Notice of Meeting.

As the Order makes no provision as to who shall be convener of the first meeting of the Distress Committee, it will be necessary for the Council to appoint a convener. "This meeting should be held as soon as possible after the appointment of the Committee." [L.G.B.C.L., 20th September, 1905.]

As the Committee have at their first meeting to appoint a Chairman (Article VIII.), the notice convening the meeting should mention that a Chairman of the Committee will have to be appointed. A Vice-Chairman is mentioned in Article X, but he need not be appointed at the first meeting.

Chairman
of Distress
Committee.

ARTICLE VIII.   Each Distress Committee at their first meeting, and thereafter as occasion requires, shall appoint one of their number to be Chairman.

The term of office of the Chairman shall be such as the Distress Committee appoint, but if during that term the Chairman ceases (as the case may be) to be a member of the Council by whom he was appointed, or of the Board of Guardians by whom he was selected for appointment as a member of the Distress Committee, or ceases to be a member of the Distress Committee from any other cause, the Distress Committee shall forthwith proceed to appoint another person to be Chairman for the rest of the term.

NOTE.—As to appointment of a Vice-Chairman see Article X., and for expression "forthwith" see Note (1) to Article III. of the London Order.

Meetings.

ARTICLE IX.   After the first meeting all ordinary meetings of a Distress Committee shall be held at such times and places as are appointed by the Distress Committee.

An extraordinary meeting of a Distress Committee shall be summoned by the Chairman on his own responsibility, or on the receipt of a requisition in writing from any three members of the Distress Committee, but no business other than that specified in the summons for the extraordinary meeting shall be transacted at that meeting.

ARTICLE X. Every question at a Meeting of a Distress Committee shall be decided by a majority of votes of the members present and voting on that question, and in the case of equality of votes the person presiding at the meeting shall have a second or casting vote.

The quorum of a Distress Committee shall be one-third of the whole number of members of the Distress Committee.

A Distress Committee may appoint from among their members such and so many Committees, either of a general or special nature, and consisting of such number of persons as the Distress Committee think fit, for any purposes which, in their opinion, would be better regulated and managed by means of Committees, and may delegate, with or without any restrictions or conditions, any of their powers and duties; and the quorum, proceedings, and place of meeting of any Committee shall be such as may be determined by regulations of the Distress Committee.

Subject to the provisions of the Act, and of any Regulations under the Act, a Distress Committee may regulate their own procedure, and may make rules with respect to the appointment and duties of a Vice-Chairman and generally with respect to the transaction and management of their business.

NOTE.—As to removal of any difficulty arising with respect to first meeting, see Article XI., also see Notes to Articles XIII. and XIV. in London Order.

F

Removal of difficulties.

ARTICLE XI.   If any difference or difficulty arises with respect to the establishment of a Distress Committee or with respect to the appointment of members of a Distress Committee, or with respect to the number of members of a Distress Committee whom a Council may appoint after selection by a Board of Guardians, or with respect to the first meeting of a Distress Committee, We may, by Order, do anything which appears to Us to be necessary or expedient for the determination of any such difference or the removal of any such difficulty or for the proper establishment of a Distress Committee or for the proper holding of the first meeting of a Distress Committee.

Short title.

ARTICLE XII.   This Order may be cited as "The Urban Distress Committees (Unemployed Workmen) Order, 1905."

SCHEDULE.

Boroughs.

		Number of Members appointed.			
Borough.	Poor Law Union wholly or partly in Borough.	From Council	From Guardians.	From Persons experienced in Relief of Distress	Total.
Aston Manor ...	Aston	12	8	5	25
Barrow-in-Furness..	Barrow-in-Furness.	12	8	5	25
Birkenhead ...	Birkenhead ...	14	10	6	30
Birmingham	{ Aston ...	—	5	—	—
	Birmingham ...	—	7	—	—
	Kings Norton ...	—	2	—	—
		18	14	8	40
Blackburn... ...	Blackburn ...	14	10	6	30
Bolton	Bolton	14	10	6	30
Bootle	West Derby ...	12	8	5	25
Bournemouth ...	Christchurch ...	12	8	5	25
Bradford ...	{ Bradford ...	—	10	—	—
	North Bierley...	—	2	—	—
		16	12	7	35
Brighton ...	{ Brighton ...	—	8	—	—
	Steyning ...	—	2	—	—
		14	10	6	30
Bristol	Bristol	16	12	7	35
Burnley	Burnley... ...	12	8	5	25
Burton-upon-Trent.	Burton-upon-Trent.	12	8	5	25
Bury	Bury	12	8	5	25

Schedule—Boroughs—

Borough.	Poor Law Union wholly or partly in Borough.	From Council	From Guardians.	From Persons experienced in Relief of Distress	Total.
			Number of Members appointed.		
Cardiff ...	... Cardiff	14	10	6	30
Coventry ...	... Coventry ...	12	8	5	25
Croydon ...	... Croydon ...	14	10	6	30
Derby ...	... Derby ...	14	10	6	30
Devonport ...	... Devonport ...	12	8	5	25
East Ham ...	... West Ham ...	12	8	5	25
Gateshead ...	... Gateshead ...	14	10	6	30
Great Yarmouth {	East and West Flegg.	—	1	—	—
	Great Yarmouth	—	7	—	—
		12	8	5	25
Grimsby ...	... Grimsby ...	12	8	5	25
Halifax ...	... Halifax	14	10	6	30
Hanley ...	... Stoke-upon-Trent.	12	8	5	25
Hastings ... {	Battle ...	—	1	—	—
	Hastings ...	—	7	—	—
		12	8	5	25
Hornsey ...	... Edmonton ...	12	8	5	25
Huddersfield	... Huddersfield ...	12	8	5	25
Ipswich ...	... Ipswich... ...	12	8	5	25
Kingston-upon-Hull. {	Kingston-upon-Hull.	—	4	—	—
	Sculcoates ...	—	8	—	—
		16	12	7	35
Leeds ... {	Bramley ...	—	2	—	—
	Holbeck ...	—	1	—	—
	Hunslet... ...	—	2	—	—
	Leeds	—	9	—	—
		18	14	8	40

Schedule—Boroughs.—

Borough.	Poor Law Union wholly or partly in Borough.		Number of Members appointed.			
		From Council	From Guardians.	From Persons experienced in Relief of Distress	Total
Leicester ...	... Leicester ...	16	12	7	35
Liverpool ...	{ Liverpool ...	—	5	—	—
	Toxteth Park ...	—	2	—	—
	West Derby ...	—	7	—	—
		18	14	8	40
Manchester...	{ Chorlton ...	—	6	—	—
	Manchester ...	—	5	—	—
	Prestwich ...	—	3	—	—
		18	14	8	40
Middlesbrough ...	... Middlesbrough ..	12	8	5	25
Newcastle-upon-Tyne.	{ Newcastle-upon-Tyne.	—	11	—	—
	Tynemouth ...	—	1	—	—
		16	12	7	35
Newport (Mon.) ...	Newport (Mon.)	12	8	5	25
Northampton	{ Hardingstone ...	—	1	—	—
	Northampton ...	—	7	—	—
		12	8	5	25
Norwich ...	... Norwich ...	14	10	6	30
Nottingham ...	... Nottingham ...	16	12	7	35
Oldham ...	... Oldham... ...	14	10	6	30
Plymouth ...	... Plymouth ...	14	10	6	30
Portsmouth ...	... Portsmouth ...	14	10	6	30
Preston ...	... Preston	14	10	6	30
Reading ...	... Reading ...	12	8	5	25
Rochdale ...	... Rochdale ...	12	8	5	25

Schedule—Boroughs—

Borough.	Poor Law Union wholly or partly in Borough.	Number of Members appointed.			
		From Council	From Guardians.	From Persons experienced in Relief of Distress	Total.
Rotherham ...	Rotherham ...	12	8	5	25
St. Helens ...	Prescot	12	8	5	25
Salford ...	Salford	16	12	7	35
Sheffield ...	Ecclesall Bierlow.	—	6	—	—
	Sheffield ...	—	8	—	—
		18	14	8	40
Smethwick...	King's Norton...	12	8	5	25
Southampton	Southampton ...	—	6	—	—
	South Stoneham.	—	4	—	—
		14	10	6	30
South Shields	South Shields ...	14	10	6	30
Stockport ...	Stockport ...	12	8	5	25
Stockton-on-Tees ...	Stockton ...	12	8	5	25
Sunderland	Sunderland ...	14	10	6	30
Swansea ...	Swansea ...	12	8	5	25
Tynemouth	Tynemouth ...	12	8	5	25
Walsall ...	Walsall ...	12	8	5	25
Warrington	Warrington ...	12	8	5	25
West Bromwich ...	West Bromwich.	12	8	5	25
West Ham...	West Ham ...	16	12	7	35
West Hartlepool....	Hartlepool ...	12	8	5	25
Wigan ...	Wigan	12	8	5	25
Wolverhampton ...	Wolverhampton.	12	8	5	25
York ...	York	12	8	5	25

URBAN DISTRICTS.

Urban District.	Poor Law Union wholly or partly in Urban District.	Number of Members appointed.			
		From Council	From Guardians.	From Persons experienced in Relief of Distress	Total.
Handsworth (Stafford).	West Bromwich	12	8	5	25
King's Norton and Northfield...	King's Norton...	12	8	5	25
Leyton	... West Ham	12	8	5	25
Merthyr Tydfil ...	... Merthyr Tydfil..	12	8	5	25
Rhondda	... Pontypridd ...	14	10	6	30
Tottenham... ...	... Edmonton ...	14	10	6	30
Wallasey	... Birkenhead ...	12	8	5	25
Walthamstow ...	... West Ham ...	12	8	5	25
Willesden	... Willesden ...	14	10	6	30

Given under the Seal of Office of the Local Government Board, this Twentieth day of September, in the year One thousand nine hundred and five.

G. W. BALFOUR,

President.

L. S.

S. B. PROVIS,

Secretary.

"THE REGULATIONS (ORGANISATION FOR UNEMPLOYED) 1905."

Introductory Note.

"The Organisation (Unemployed Workmen) Establishment Order, 1905" applies to London. "The Urban Distress Committees (Unemployed Workmen) Establishment Order, 1905" applies to every Municipal Borough and Urban District outside London with a population according to last census of not less than 50,000.

The following Regulations prescribing the "Powers and Duties of Distress Committees and of the Central Body" apply not only to the areas mentioned in the two aforesaid Orders, but as will be seen from the Bodies to whom the Regulations are addressed, to the whole of England and Wales. Such Regulations, however, are not applicable in all areas alike; for instance, they include provisions relating to Special Committees (Section 2 (3) of the Act) where a Central Body or Distress Committee under the Act have not been established.

𝕿𝖔 𝖊𝖛𝖊𝖗𝖞 𝕮𝖊𝖓𝖙𝖗𝖆𝖑 𝕭𝖔𝖉𝖞 under the Unemployed Workmen Act, 1905 ;—

To every Distress Committee and to every Special Committee under that Act ;—

To the London County Council ;—

To the Councils of all other Administrative Counties ;—

To the Mayor, Aldermen, and Commons of the City of London in Common Council assembled ; —

To the Mayor, Aldermen, and Councillors of each Metropolitan Borough ;—

To the Council of every Municipal Borough or Urban District to which the said Act applies ;—

And to all others whom it may concern.

WHEREAS for the purposes of organisation with a view to the provision of employment or assistance for unemployed workmen in proper cases the Unemployed Workmen Act, 1905, provides for the establishment of Central Bodies and Distress Committees for London and for certain Boroughs, Urban Districts, and other areas, and for the constitution of Special Committees by the Councils of Counties and County Boroughs in certain cases ;

And whereas by Section 4 (3) of the said Act it is enacted as follows :—

"(3) The Local Government Board may make "regulations for carrying into effect this Act, "and may by those regulations, amongst other "things, provide—

"(a) for regulating, subject to the provisions "of this Act, the conditions under which any "application may be entertained by a Distress "Committee under this Act, and the conditions "under which a Central Body may aid emigration "or removal, or provide or contribute towards the "provision of work under this Act, and otherwise "for regulating the manner in which any duties "under this Act are to be performed or powers "exercised by any Central Body or Distress "Committee or Special Committee under this "Act ; and

"(b) for authorising the establishment, with "the consent of the Local Government Board, of "farm colonies by a Central Body established "under this Act, and the provision, with the like "consent, by such a body of temporary accommoda- "tion for persons for whom work upon the land is "provided ; and

"(c) for authorising and regulating the "acquisition by a Central Body of land by "agreement for the purposes of this Act, and "the disposal of any land so acquired ; and

" (*d*) for the employment of officers and
" provision of offices, and for enabling any
" inspector of the Local Government Board to
" attend the meeting of any body or committee
" established under this Act ; and

" (*e*) for authorising the acceptance of any
" money or property by a Central Body established
" under this Act, and for regulating the adminis-
" tration of any money or property so acquired ;
" and

" (*f*) for the payment of any receipts of a
" Central Body to the Central Fund, and for the
" apportionment, if necessary, of those receipts
" between the Voluntary Contribution Account
" and the Rate Contribution Account of that
" Fund ; and

" (*g*) for the audit of the accounts of any
" Central Body established under this Act in the
" same manner and subject to the same provisions
" as to any matters incidental to the audit or
" consequential thereon as the accounts of a
" County Council ; and

" (*h*) for enforcing the payment of contri-
" butions by any Councils liable to make such
" contributions in pursuance of this Act, and for
" authorising and regulating the borrowing of
" money by a Central Body established under
" this Act ; and

" (*i*) for facilitating the co-operation of any
" body or committee having powers under this
" Act for any area with any other body or
" committee, or with any local authority, and
" the provision of assistance by one such body or
" committee to another; and

" (*k*) for applying, with the necessary adapta-
" tions, to a Distress Committee having the powers
" of a Central Body regulations relating to a
" Central Body; and

" (*l*) for the holding of local inquiries by the
" Local Government Board for the purposes of
" this Act, and for requiring returns to be made
" to the Board by any body or committee having
" powers under this Act; and

" (*m*) for the application for the purposes of
" this Act, as respects any matters to be dealt
" with by the Regulations, of any provision in
" any Act of Parliament dealing with the like
" matters, with any necessary modifications or
" adaptations."

NOW THEREFORE, for carrying into effect the
Unemployed Workmen Act, 1905, We, the Local
Government Board, in the exercise of Our powers in
that behalf, Do hereby make the following Regulations,
that is to say : —

ARTICLE I. (1) In these Regulations, unless the contrary intention appears—

Interpretation and effect of Regulations

(*a*) Words importing the masculine gender include females;

(*b*) Words in the singular include the plural, and words in the plural include the singular;

(*c*) The expression "the Act" means the Unemployed Workmen Act, 1905;

(*d*) The expression "Local Exchange" means a Labour Exchange, or an Employment Register (whether in the form of a Labour Bureau, or in any other form) having for its object the supply of information either by the keeping of registers or otherwise respecting employers who desire to engage workpeople and workpeople who seek engagement or employment; and

(*e*) The expression "Central Exchange" means a Labour Exchange having for its object the co-ordination, or circulation of, or other dealing with information collected by two or more Local Exchanges.

(2) These Regulations shall have effect subject to the provisions of the Act.

Conditions
affecting
applications
to Distress
Committee,
and cases
referred to
Central
Body.

ARTICLE II.   (1) The conditions under which an application may be entertained by a Distress Committee under the Act shall be as follows:—

(i) An applicant shall make his application in person to an officer, or to a member, or to any other person authorised by the Distress Committee to receive and investigate applications; and shall also, if so required, attend, for the purpose of his application, any such meeting of the Distress Committee or of a Committee of the Distress Committee, as the Distress Committee or Committee appoint.

(ii) An applicant shall answer all questions put to him and shall supply all such information as may be required by the Distress Committee, by a Committee of the Distress Committee, or by an officer, a member, or any other person authorised by the Distress Committee with respect to the applicant or any of his dependants, or with respect to any other matters concerning which the Distress Committee or the Committee, or the officer, member, or other person may need information for the purposes of the Act or of any Regulations under the Act.

(iii) An officer, a member, or any other person authorised by the Distress Committee to receive and investigate applications, shall visit and make inquiries at the home of the applicant for the verification of the statements

of the applicant, and shall also, where the
circumstances so require, with the same object,
communicate with a Board of Guardians or
with any other body, authority, or person able
to supply useful information with respect to
the applicant.

(1) When Applications are to be received.

In the Circular Letter, sent with the Regulations, to
" London, City and Metropolitan Boroughs " (10th October,
1905) the Local Government Board state that :—

" Section 1 (2) of the Act directs that the Distress Committee shall make themselves acquainted with the conditions of
labour within their area, *and, when so required by the Central
Body,* shall receive, inquire into, and discriminate between any
applications made to them from persons unemployed.

" It will be observed that this latter duty is only to be
performed by the Distress Committee *when they are required so
to do by the Central Body.* The Board think that the Committee
should not be required to receive applications irrespective of
the state of trade or employment which may prevail at any
given time, and that when the Central Body impose this requirement upon a Distress Committee they should do so for a period
fixed by them according to the circumstances then existing.

In the Circular Letter, of the same date, sent with the
Regulations, to the Councils of populous Borough and Urban
Districts in the Provinces, the Board observed that:—

" The Distress Committee established by the Order will
have the same powers and duties, so far as applicable, as are
given by the Act to the Distress Committees and Central Body
in London, and Article XXI. of the Regulations provides that,
so far as they relate to a Central Body, the Regulations shall
apply, with the necessary adaptations, to every Distress
Committee having the powers of a Central Body.

" It will be the duty of the Distress Committee to make
themselves acquainted with the conditions of labour within their
area, and also to receive, inquire into, and discriminate between
any applications made to them from persons unemployed. As
regards this latter duty, the Board think that it will be
competent to the Committee to determine from time to time
whether applications should be received by them, regard being
had to the state of trade or employment then prevalent, and to
fix a period during which applications will be received."

Art. II.—Note—

(2) *Conditions affecting applications to Distress Committees.*

Section 4 (3). (*a*) of the Act empowers the Local Government Board to make Regulations "for regulating, subject to the provisions of the Act, the conditions under which any application may be entertained by a Distress Committee under this Act." As to these conditions see notes below so far as they relate to Article II.

(3) *The minimum questions to applicant.*

For the minimum of questions which an applicant may be required to answer see the Record Paper given in the Schedule in the Regulations.

(4) *Unemployed Workwomen as well as Unemployed Men may apply.*

Unemployed workwomen, although not mentioned in the Act, are brought in by the operation of "The Interpretation Act, 1889" (52 and 53 Vic., c. 63) Section 1 (1), (*a*), where it is enacted that "words importing the masculine gender shall include females unless the contrary intention appears." Article I. (1), (*a*), of the Regulations is in accordance.

(5) *Applicant's "Dependants."*

Neither the Act nor the Regulations define the expression "Dependants." Under "Lord Campbell's Act" (9 and 10 Vic., c. 93)—an Act for compensating the families of persons killed by accidents—the expression "dependants" means wife, husband, father, mother, grandfather, grandmother, step-father, step-mother, son, daughter, grandson, granddaughter, step-son, and step-daughter (Sections 2 and 5). Under the Poor Law Acts liability for maintenance attaches to a person, male or female, for chargeable wife or husband, parents, children, and grandchildren ["Poor Law Relief Act, 1601" (43 Eliz., c. 2, s. 7); "Poor Law Amendment Act, 1868" (31 and 32 Vict., c. 122, s. 37); "Married Women's Property Act, 1882" (45 and 46 Vic., c. 75, s-s. 20, 21); "Poor Law Amendment Act, 1834" (4 and 5 Will. IV., c. 76, s-s. 57 and 71); "Bastardy Law Amendment Act, 1872" (35 and 36 Vic., c. 65, s. 4)]. Under "The Workmen's Compensation Act, 1897" any question as to who is a "dependant" is, in default of agreement, to be settled by arbitration. It is submitted that the term either under the Act or Regulations should be as broadly interpreted as legal or moral liability requires. It may be pointed out that question 13 of the Record Paper in the Schedule to the Regulations mentions wife, children, "and other dependants."

Art. II.—NOTE—

(6) *Delegation of Applications to Sub-Committee.*

Article XIV. of the London Organisation Order and Article X. of the Provincial Organisation Order enable a Distress Committee to delegate "with or without any restrictions or conditions, any of their powers and duties" to a Committee or Committees appointed from their members. In the Circular Letters accompanying the Regulations such Committees are termed Sub-Committees.

(iv) In the case of each applicant the Distress Committee shall call for and consider the Record Paper which, in pursuance of these Regulations, has been provided and is in use in relation to the case, and shall satisfy themselves:

(*a*) That the applicant is of good character;

(*b*) That he has not from any source sufficient means to maintain himself and his dependants;

(*c*) That he is not, and has not been during the period of twelve months immediately preceding the date of the application, in receipt of relief (other than medical relief) at the cost of the poor rate;

(*d*) That he has not in two successive periods of twelve months immediately preceding the date of the application, been employed on work provided by a Central Body, or on work towards the provision of which a Central Body have contributed; and

(*e*) That his case is in other respects one which the Distress Committee, with due observance of the requirements of the Act, may properly entertain.

G

Art. II.—Note—

(1) *Class of Applicants to whom the Act applies.*

In the Circular Letter, sent with the Regulations, to "London, City, and any Metropolitan Boroughs," on 10th October, 1905, the Local Government Board state that—

"The Act [Section 1 (2)] expressly provides that a Distress Committee shall not entertain an application from any person unless they are satisfied that he has resided in London for such period, not being less than 12 months, immediately before the application as the Central Body fix as a residential qualification. Under Paragraph (iv.) (c) of Article II. (1) of the Regulations, it will be the duty of the Committee to satisfy themselves that this prohibition is not infringed, and also that the conditions mentioned in Section 1 (3) of the Act are fulfilled, viz. :—

> (1) That the applicant is honestly desirous of obtaining work.
>
> (2) That he is temporarily unable to do so from exceptional causes over which he has no control ; and
>
> (3) That his case is capable of more suitable treatment under the Act than under the Poor Law."

Similar observations to the foregoing are made by the Board in their Circular Letter of the same date, sent with the Regulations, to the Councils of populous Boroughs and Urban Districts in the Provinces. In such areas the area of residence is to be the area of the Distress Committee, and the Distress Committee are to fix the residential qualification, though not at less than 12 months [As to discrimination in cases see Note to Article II. (2)].

(2) *Poor Law Relief Disqualification.*

An application from any person—male or female—who is, or has been during a period of 12 months (calendar months—Art. II.) immediately preceding date of the application, in receipt of Poor Law Relief (other than Medical Relief) is not to be entertained by the Distress Committee. On the face this Regulation may appear harsh, seeing that (1) Section 1 (7) of the Act preserves the franchise to persons who may be assisted ; and (2) that food provided to school children under the recently issued Order of the Local Government Board *re* Underfed School Children is relief to the father. "Poor Law Amendment Act, 1834" (4 and 5 Will. IV., c. 76, s. 56). The justification for the Regulation apparently lies in the fact that a status of irremovability [See Note 2 Article II. (2)] may be gained by residence

ART. II.—NOTE—

for the aggregate period of a year, made up of shorter periods during which no relief is received [Ipswich Union v. West Ham 52 L. T. 469] therefore if the Distress Committee were to entertain applications from persons who, though they had been resident in the district for more than twelve months, had not obtained a status of irremovability, and such persons received assistance by being found work, that assistance might enable them to get the status of irremovability with the consequence that should such persons subsequently become chargeable as paupers the Board of Guardians in whose area the status had been obtained would not be able to shift the charge to the Union in which the Parish of settlement was situate.

Medical Relief is defined by "The Medical Relief Disqualification Removal Act, 1885" (18 and 49 Vict., c. 46, s. 4) as "all Medical and Surgical attendance, and all matters and things supplied by, or on the recommendation of the Medical Officer having authority to give such attendance and recommendation at the expense of any Poor Rate."

(3) "*Case of more suitable treatment under the Act than under the Poor Law.*" (Act, Sect. 1 (3)).

Applicants who are not disqualified by reason of relief may be considered by the Distress Committee more suitable for Poor Law treatment than assistance under the Act (Section 1 (3)).

It is advisable that Distress Committees should ascertain whether in their respective districts the "Out Relief Regulation Order," or "Out-door Relief Prohibitory Order" is in force. In places where the latter Order is in force the Guardians can only relieve able-bodied men, with or without families, with an order for the Workhouse. The Order makes provision that Out-door relief may be given in certain cases, but as may be inferred from what has been already stated relief of the ordinary case of unemployed able-bodied must be "wholly in the Workhouse." See Appendix.

(2) The case of an applicant as to whom the Distress Committee have satisfied themselves—

(a) that in the past he has been regularly employed, has resided in their area for a continuous period of twelve months at the least and has been well-conducted and thrifty, (*b*) that at the time of his application he has a wife, child, or other dependant,

      (*c*) that, in respect of age and physical ability, he is qualified for such work as the Distress Committee may be able to obtain, and also

      (*d*) that, in other respects, the case of the applicant is one which may be entertained in accordance with the conditions prescribed by this Regulation,

shall be treated by the Distress Committee in preference to cases of a different character.

(1) *Discrimination by Committee and Preference as to Cases.*

    Section 1 (2) of the Act directs that the Committee shall discriminate between any applications made to them. In their Circular Letters with the Regulations (10th October, 1905), the Local Government Board point out that :—"It will always be in the discretion of the Committee whether they will or will not entertain an application made to them by a person who satisfies the prescribed conditions, but Article II. (2) provides that certain cases shall be treated by the Committee in preference to others of a different character." They further point out that "A case to be treated preferentially" must be that of an applicant as to whom the Committee have not only satisfied themselves that he complies with the conditions mentioned in Section 1 (3) of the Act but have also satisfied themselves that he fulfils the conditions in Article II. (2) of the Regulations. This matter of discrimination and preference was keenly debated in both Houses of Parliament, and the President of the Local Government Board (Mr. Gerald Balfour), whilst laying great emphasis on the conditions mentioned in Section 1 (3) of the Act, said that his meaning would be made more clear by reference to Mr. Charles Booth's classification of the inhabitants of the poorer districts of London :— A, the lowest, roughly corresponding to those who were hopelessly unemployed ; B, those who were casually employed ; C, those with intermittent employment ; D, regular workers at low wages ; and E, regular workers at standard rates of payment. It was not intended that work should be provided for classes A and B or generally for class C.

Art. II.—Note—

In the House of Lords, Lord Balfour of Burleigh asked the Marquis of Lansdowne, in charge of the Bill in the House—(*a*) How long, in the opinion of the Local Government Board, would a man have to be out of work before he was regarded as a fit applicant for the benefit of the Act? (*b*) Would the following classes be also considered fit applicants?—(1) Men refusing work because it was not paid for according to the standard rate of trade-union remuneration; (2) Men on strike; and (3) Men regularly short of work during a portion of the year, but getting good wages for a considerable part of the year. The Marquis of Lansdowne answered that, subject to the provisions of the Act and Regulations, the decisions of the Local Body must depend upon the circumstances of each particular case; but his answer, in relation to men invariably well-occupied and paid during a part of the year, and regularly short of work in winter months was in the negative. The Marquis also stated that the question was considered when the Bill was being prepared and the words (Section 1 (3)) "from exceptional causes over which he has no control" were inserted (Parliamentary Debates).

(2) *Residential qualification for Application.*

While the period under the present Act may not be "less than twelve months, immediately before the application" [Act, Sect. 1 (2)], the Central Body—or Distress Committee having the power of a Central Body—may fix a longer period than 12 months. "Month" means "Calendar Month" [Interpretation Act, 1889, 52 and 53 Vict. 63. Sect. 3]. There was no residential qualification inserted in the present measure as originally introduced. It was inserted on representation that there should be a qualification equal to that required to give a person a status of irremovability under the Poor Law, which is 12 months unbroken residence without relief [Union Chargeability Act, 1865, 28 and 29 Vict. c. 79. Sect. 8]. In connection with Poor Removal Law it has been held that there is no break in residence under the following circumstances:—(1) Absence for a merely temporary purpose, with an intention to return [R. v. Stapleton, 22 L.J. M. C. 102, per Crompton J.; Wellington v. Whitechurch, 32 L.J. M. C. 189. 27 J.P. 646] and (2) Absence to do work under a contract where there is intention to return upon completion of contract [R. v. Brighton Poor Directors, 24 L.J. M. C. 41, 24 L.T. (N.S.) 138]. Absence while seeking work, but maintaining family while away and afterwards returning, has been held not to necessarily constitute a break in residence [R. v. Tacolneston, 18 L.J. M. C. 44; R. v. St. Marylebone, 20 L.J. M. C. 173].

ART. II.—NOTES—

As to area in which residential qualification is necessary
see Page 98. It should be understood that while residence must
be continuous in the area of the Central Body or Distress
Committee it need not be continuous in the same dwelling within
the area.

Owing to the terms of Sect. 1 (2) of the Act, oddly enough,
a man who returns to his birthplace after an absence of twelve
months will not in that place be able to have the benefits of the
Act until he has obtained the twelve months' residential qualification, in other words, he will be in the position of a stranger.

(3) *What the Committee may do to assist Applicants.*

"If the Distress Committee are satisfied that the case of
an applicant is one in which the prescribed conditions are complied with, they may endeavour to obtain work for him. If,
however, they think that the case is one for treatment by the
Central Body rather than by themselves they may refer the case
to that Body, and in this way the Distress Committee will be able
to deal with the cases of applicants for whom they are unable to
obtain work, but for whom they think that work should, if
possible, be provided. In no case, however, will the Committee
have any power to provide or contribute towards the provision of
work for any unemployed person, i.e., either to employ him themselves, or to make any payment in respect of his employment by
others" [L.G.B.C.L., 10th October, 1905, London, City and Metro-
litan Boroughs]. The Act, Sect. 1 (3), provides for Reference to
Central Body. Outside London, in any area, where there is a
Distress Committee and no Central Body, the Distress Committee will have the power of a Central Body [Act, Sect. 2 (1);
Regulations, Article XXI].

(4) *Dependants.*

See Note 5 to Article II. (1) (i), (ii), (iii).

(3) In any case of an unemployed person referred
to a Central Body by a Distress Committee, this Regulation shall, where the circumstances so require, apply
with the substitution of references to the Central Body,
and an officer, a member, or any other person authorised
by the Central Body for references to the Distress
Committee, and an officer, a member, or any other
person authorised by the Distress Committee, and

with such other modifications and adaptations as are
necessary to render this Regulation applicable to the
duties to be performed and the powers to be exercised
by the Central Body :

Provided that it shall be within the discretion of
the Central Body to investigate anew the facts of any
case referred to them by a Distress Committee, but
that nothing in this Regulation shall require the Central Body to do so :

Provided also that where the Central Body think fit
to require a Distress Committee to make a further
investigation of the facts of any case referred by the
Distress Committee to the Central Body, the Distress
Committee shall forthwith comply with the requisition
of the Central Body, and report the results to the Central Body.

NOTE.— Art. II. (3) The Central Body should not deal with any
case referred to them by the Distress Committee, unless it is
one which comes within the provisions prescribed in Article I.
See Article VI. (4).

(4) Where a Distress Committee or a Central Body
are satisfied that the answer to a question put to an
applicant, or that the information supplied by an applicant with respect to any matter which, in their opinion,
is material, is false to the knowledge of the applicant,
the Distress Committee or the Central Body shall make
and keep a suitable record of the case.

Art. II.

A person whose case is so recorded shall, until, for good cause shown to them, the Distress Committee or the Central Body cancel the record, cease to be qualified to receive assistance from a Distress Committee or a Central Body.

NOTE.—Art. II. (4) No penalty is prescribed in the Act for wilful false statement made by applicant, therefore the only penalty is the disqualification laid down by this Regulation [See Article XXI].

Emigration.   ARTICLE III. (1) The conditions under which a Central Body may aid the emigration of an unemployed person and any of his dependants shall be as follows:—

The Central Body shall satisfy themselves that the unemployed person and any of his dependants whose emigration is to be aided will be conveyed to and received at the place of destination in circumstances which will secure or facilitate the immediate fulfilment of the condition that the unemployed person shall be put in a position to obtain regular work, or other means of supporting himself and any of his dependants who accompany him.

(2) The case of an applicant for assistance who satisfies the Central Body that, in respect of age, physical ability, and past employment, he is qualified for employment in agriculture, including horticulture, forestry, and the use of land for any purpose of husbandry, the keeping and breeding of live stock, or the growth of fruit or vegetables, shall be treated by the Central Body in preference to cases of a different character.

Art. III.

(3) The Central Body shall, at the end of every month, report to the Local Government Board in a form to be furnished by the Local Government Board all such particulars as are indicated in the form in relation to every person who during the month has been aided to emigrate.

(1) *Colonial and Foreign Immigration Laws.*

In deciding to aid emigration of any case the most rigid adherence to the terms of the regulation of Article III. (1) is absolutely necessary by reason of the *Measures adopted for the Restriction and Control of Immigration in Foreign Countries and in British Colonies.*

The Measures referred to are set out in the recently issued Report of the Royal Commission on Alien Immigration, which may be obtained from Messrs. Eyre and Spottiswoode, East Harding Street, Fleet Street, E.C. (price sixpence). See further under Note (2).

(2) *Emigration under Poor Law and the Local Government Act,* 1888.

There are extensive provisions made in these Acts with respect to Emigration. They are fully set out in the *"Emigration Statutes and General Handbook"* issued by the Emigrants' Information Office, 31, Broadway, Westminster, S.W. The handbook is edited by Mr. Walter Paton, M.A. (Barrister-at-Law), and contains exhaustive information, *inter alia,* on Colonial Statutes to restrict undesirable immigration. It also contains a list of British Emigration Societies. The handbook may be obtained from Messrs. Wyman and Sons Ltd., Fetter Lane, E.C., or direct from the Emigrants' Information Office (price threepence).

(3) *Dependants.*

See Note 5 to Article II. (1).
See Article XXI.

ARTICLE IV. The conditions under which a Central Body may aid the removal to another area of an unemployed person and any of his dependants shall be as follows:—

Removal

(i) The unemployed person and a dependant of the unemployed person shall be aided to remove only to an area within the limits of England and Wales:

(ii) The Central Body shall satisfy themselves that the unemployed person whose removal to another area is to be aided will, on reaching the place of destination in that area, be put at once in a position to obtain regular work or other means of supporting himself and any of his dependants who accompany him, and that suitable dwelling accommodation for the person or persons to be removed can be provided at the place of destination:

(iii) The Central Body shall also satisfy themselves that the regular work which the unemployed person will be in a position to obtain at the place of destination will be of such duration, or that the facilities for other regular employment will be such as to afford every reasonable expectation that the person or persons whose removal is to be aided will not become chargeable to the poor rate at any time during a period of twelve months after the removal.

(1) *The restriction and conditions in the Regulations.*

Section 1 (5) of the Act legalises assistance by way of removal to another area subject to Regulations made by the Local Government Board (Section 4 (3), (a)). The restrictions in the foregoing Regulation are necessary to prevent the practical repeal of Section 6 of the " Poor Removal Act, 1846 "

Art. IV.—Note—

(9 and 10 Vict., c. 66) where it is enacted that "If any officer of any Parish or Union do contrary to law, with intent to cause any poor person to become chargeable to any parish to which such person was not then chargeable, convey any poor person out of the parish for which such officer acts, or cause or procure any poor person to be so conveyed, or give directly or indirectly any money, relief, or assistance, or afford, or procure to be afforded any facility for such conveyance, or make any offer, or promise, or use any threat to induce any poor person to depart from such parish, and if, in consequence of such conveyance or departure, any poor person become chargeable to any parish to which he was not then chargeable, such officer, on conviction thereof before any two justices, shall forfeit and pay for every such offence any sum not exceeding five pounds nor less than forty shillings."

The restriction in the Regulations are not only prohibitive of "dumping" the unemployed in other areas, but the conditions imposed are such that the person whose removal is aided shall not be likely to become at any time a charge to the Rates in his new place of domicile, and certainly not so before he or she has there obtained a status of irremovability under the Poor Law. [See Note 2 to Article II. (2)].

(2) *How the Central Body, or Distress Committee, as the case may be are to " satisfy themselves."*

One way in which this may be done is by personal investigations made by their own officer in the district to which removal is proposed. [See Article XI.]

(3) *No Consent of the Local Government Board required to either Emigration or Removal: Agreement of Person to repay expenditure.*

"No consent on the part of the Board will be necessary either to emigration or removal. It may be that in some instances an unemployed person who is assisted either to emigrate or to remove to another area may be willing to agree to recoup the Central Body all or part of the sum expended by them in assisting him. It will be competent for the Central Body to enter into any agreement necessary for this purpose, without any regulation being made on the subject [L.G.B. C.Ls. 10th Oct., 1905]." [See Article XXI.]

(4) *Dependants.*

See Note 5 to Art. II. (1).

Conditions
affecting
assistance
by Central
Body in the
form of
temporary
work.

ARTICLE V.   The conditions under which a Central Body may provide or contribute towards the provision of work under the Act shall be as follows :—

(i) Where the Central Body provide or contribute towards the provision of temporary work for any person, the Central Body shall employ or arrange for the employment of the applicant on such terms as will enable them to enforce, and they shall, as occasion requires, enforce the observance of the following restrictions, namely :—

NOTE.—
    Article V. (1) In the Circular Letter of the 10th October, accompanying the Regulations to London, City and Metropolitan Boroughs, the Local Government Board referring to the restrictions in this Article state that " It is important that they should be carefully studied by the Central Body." They make the same observation in their Circular Letter of the same date to the Provincial populous Boroughs and Urban Districts, substituting therein as the case requires " Distress Committee for Central Body."

(a) That the work shall have for its object a purpose of actual and substantial utility;

NOTE.—
    Article V. (1) (a) Apparently work need not necessarily be of public utility.—See Note below under paragraph (v). as to work done for private person.

(b) That each person employed on the work shall throughout his employment be subject to effectual supervision;

(c) That each person employed on the work shall perform every task allotted to him with diligence, and shall throughout his employment attain a standard of efficiency such as, with due regard to his ordinary calling or occupation, and his age and physical ability, may properly be required of him;

(d) That each person employed on the work shall, as far as possible, be afforded continuous occupation thereon day by day, with such absence only as may be needed to facilitate his search for regular work or other means of supporting himself;

NOTE.—
Article V. (1) (d) It will be advisable for Central Body or Distress Committee as the case may be, to make a Regulation of their own as to what absence will be allowed, and that the workers should be supplied with a print of it.

(e) That where the Central Body provide or contribute towards the provision of temporary work necessitating, during a period or a succession of periods comprising in each case four consecutive days at the least, continuous absence from home of the person employed and he has a wife, child, or other dependant, the Central Body shall satisfy themselves that the cost of the lodging and maintenance of the wife, child, or other dependant will be defrayed by deduction

Art. V.

> from the remuneration of the person employed, and that he has made or will make every such agreement or arrangement as may be needed to give full effect to this restriction;

NOTE.—

Article V. (1) (e) The agreement or arrangement should be made and completed in writing at the time of the worker's engagement. The Central Body or the Distress Committee, as the case may be, should ensure an arrangement by which those in whose behalf the deduction is made will obtain the benefit of it with all due despatch and convenience so as to avoid any risk of application to the Guardians for relief. As to rate of the worker's remuneration See Condition (g). For the expression "dependants" See Note (5) to Article II. (1) (i). (ii). (iii).

> (f) That where the person employed has no wife, child, or other dependant, or has a wife, child, or other dependant, but is not employed on temporary work necessitating, during a period or a succession of periods comprising in each case four consecutive days at the least, his continuous absence from home, the total remuneration of that person for any given period of continuous work shall be less than that which would under ordinary circumstances be earned by an unskilled labourer for continuous work during the same period in the place at which the work is provided; and

NOTE.—

Article V. (1), (f), (g) In the Measure as originally introduced it was provided that the total weekly remuneration for any temporary work provided for the unemployed should "be less than that which would under ordinary circumstances be earned by an unskilled labourer for a full week's work." The Act does not contain this condition. In effect, therefore, what was

Art. V.—Note—

taken out of the Measure has been put back by the Regulations. The Local Government Board in doing so have, however, not gone outside their legislative authority [See Section 4 (3), (a)]. The restrictions imposed by the Regulations not only necessitate that the worker, irrespective of the work he does, shall be paid less than the unskilled labourer, but they also necessitate different treatment between single men and men with families who are sent to work at such distance as involves absence from home for more than four consecutive days, and men with families sent to work at such a distance, and men with families not so sent. Clearly the Central Body, or Distress Committee, as the case may be, should determine upon such a rate of remuneration as on the one hand will not be a breach of the restrictions, and yet on the other hand avoid anomalies. Taking restriction (f) with restriction (g), it is quite possible for an anomaly to arise, e.g.—If a single man and a married man are provided with temporary work at such a distance from home that absence of both from home is necessitated for a longer period than "four consecutive days," the remuneration of the single man is to be less than that of the unskilled labourer where the work is, but that of the married man is to be less than that of the unskilled labourer where the family remain. If, therefore, the remuneration of the unskilled labourer in the district where the work is provided is higher than that where the married worker's family remain, the single man, may, unless a difference is made by the Central Body or Distress Committee to correct the anomaly, receive more than the married man.

> (g) That where the person employed has a wife, child, or other dependant, and the remuneration of that person is subject to deduction for the purpose of defraying the cost of the lodging and maintenance of the wife, child, or other dependant, the total remuneration of the said person for any given period of continuous work shall be less than that which would under ordinary circumstances be earned by an unskilled labourer for continuous work during the same period in the place at which the wife, child, or other dependant is lodged and maintained.

Art. V.

(ii.) Where the Central Body contribute towards the
provision of temporary work, their contribution
shall be made on terms which will enable them
to exercise, and they shall, as occasion requires,
exercise the right to withhold the contribution
or any part of the contribution on proof to their
satisfaction that any restriction mentioned in
Condition (i.) has not been observed.

NOTE.—

Article V. (1) (ii). This should be inserted as one of the
terms of the Contract made by the Local or Public Body—See
Note below to Sub-division (v).

(iii.) Where the Central Body provide or contribute
towards the provision of temporary work in any
particular case, the Central Body shall cause
all such facilities as, in their opinion, are
reasonable to be afforded for the purpose of
putting the person for whom temporary work
has been provided in a position to obtain regular
work or other means of supporting himself.

The Central Body, when satisfied that a
person for whom temporary work has been
provided has neglected to make proper use of
the facilities afforded for the purpose of putting
him in a position to obtain regular work or
other means of supporting himself, or that the
person has, without reasonable excuse, neglected
or refused to avail himself of an offer of regular
work or of other means of supporting himself,
shall put an end to the provision of temporary
work for that person.

Art. V.—Note—

NOTE.—

Article V. (iii). The facilities to be allowed in behalf of the worker are such as are required by Sect. 1 (5) of the Act.

> (iv.) The Central Body may, in the case of a person for whom temporary work has been provided, put an end at any time to the provision of temporary work for that person, and shall in no case continue the provision of temporary work for more than sixteen weeks in any period of twelve months except with the consent of the Local Government Board.

> (v.) The Central Body shall contribute towards the provision of temporary work in those cases only in which the work will be provided by a Local Authority or Public Body.

NOTE.—

Article V. (v). On Sub-division (v). of the Article the Local Government Board in their Circular Letter of the 10th October, 1905, to the London, City and Metropolitan Boroughs, observe " That, whilst it will not be competent for the Central Body to contribute towards the provision of temporary work where work is provided by a private person, it is not intended to imply that under no circumstances is work to be done by the Central Body for a private person. But in any such case the Central Body must themselves provide the work, *i.e.*, they must be the employers and responsible for the conditions of the employment as between themselves and the persons employed.

" Where the Central Body propose to contribute towards the provision of temporary work by a Local Authority or Public Body, it would appear to be desirable that an agreement should be entered into between the Central Body and the Authority concerned, and that the agreement should contain a stipulation for some recoupment to be made to the Central Body on account of the services of the workmen in respect of whom they contribute towards the work. The value of these services should be represented by a sum which should either be fixed by the agreement itself or be determined by some easy method specified in the agreement.

H

Art. V.—Note—

"Where the Central Body are themselves the employers, but the work is for the benefit of some third party, the same general principles will apply."

The same observations are made in the Circular Letter sent to the Provincial populous Boroughs and Urban Districts on the same date, "Distress Committee" being named in that Letter for "Central Body" in the London Circular.

General Note on Above.

Women as well as men may be provided with work. See Note 4, Article II. (1) (i). (ii). (iii). Also see Article XXI. in reference to expression "Central Body."

(vi.) In every case in which the Central Body provide or contribute towards the provision of temporary work, the provision of temporary work shall be subject to this Regulation, and the conditions specified in this Regulation shall form part of the terms and conditions of the employment of any person under the Act or these Regulations.

Record Papers and Index.

ARTICLE VI. (1) A Distress Committee shall form and keep a current record of every case in which they receive, inquire into, or entertain an application under the Act.

(2) For those purposes, the Distress Committee shall provide for use in accordance with this Regulation a sufficient supply of Record Papers in the form set forth in the Schedule to this Order.

(3) All such particulars as are indicated in the Form in the Schedule to this Order and are appropriate to the circumstances of each case shall be entered, from time to time, and as soon as possible, upon the Record

Art. VI.

Paper relating to the case by an officer or by a member or by any other person authorised by the Distress Committee, by the Central Body or by a Committee of the Distress Committee or of the Central Body, according as the circumstances or any directions or regulations of the Distress Committee or of the Central Body require; and, in other respects, the Record Paper shall be used in accordance with the instructions in the said Form.

(4) The Distress Committee shall retain in their custody the Record Paper relating to every application which they receive, inquire into, or entertain under the Act, and which has not been made in a case referred under the Act to the Central Body.

Where a case is referred under the Act by the Distress Committee to the Central Body, the Record Paper relating to the case shall be transferred by the Distress Committee to the Central Body, and shall be retained in the custody of the Central Body.

(5) The Distress Committee and the Central Body shall each provide and by alteration, addition, or otherwise shall each keep at all times ready for use an Alphabetical Index to the Record Papers retained in their custody.

NOTE.—Article VI.—

The Circular Letters (10th October, 1905) of the Local Government Board sent to London, City and Metropolitan Boroughs, and to Provincial populous Boroughs and Urban Districts, with the Regulations, state that:—"It is intended that there shall be a *Record Paper for each Case.*" They further state (Circular to the Provinces) that the Record Paper is *to be kept up to date.* By "keeping up to date" should be understood that after the original decision or action on the case, which must be duly recorded, punctual record must be made of the "after history of the case" [See part II. of the Record Paper in the Schedule], as such history becomes known. The

Art. VI.—Note—

Board in such Circular Letters point out that an Alphabetical Index is required, " In order that the Record Paper in any particular case may be readily found." The Transfer of Record Paper to Central Body (second paragraph of sub-division (4) will be necessary for the assistance of the Central Body [See sub-division (3) of Article II.]. Of course where a Distress Committee have the powers of a Central Body [See Article XXI.] no transfer is necessary.

Register.

ARTICLE VII. A Distress Committee and a Central Body shall each keep a Register.

The Register shall be in such form as the Distress Committee or the Central Body think fit, subject to the condition that the form shall be so arranged as to be suitable for recording the names and addresses, and the trade, calling, employment or occupation of each person from whom the Distress Committee have received an application, and such other particulars as the Distress Committee or the Central Body, as the case may be, cause to be extracted from any Record Paper which relates to the application.

Note—Article VII.

In the Circular Letters, mentioned in Note to Article VI., the Local Government Board say that " It will be in the discretion of the Committee to determine the form of the Register "—so long, of course, as it is so arranged as to be suitable for the recording of particulars required by the Regulation. The Regulation is that " The Register shall be in such form as the Distress Committee or Central Body think fit, subject, etc." The Regulation is worded so that both Distress Committee and Central Body may each have their own form. In actual working this may be necessary as the Central Body may have to deal with cases migrating from one Committee to another in the area of the Central Body. It is advisable that the form of Register should be the same for all Committees within the area of a Central Body. For the Central Body's power of co-ordination, see Section I. (4) of the Act. The Board point out [London Circular] that the Distress Committee on Reference of case to Central Body will have to part with the Record Paper, but by means of the Register should be able to refer to circumstances of any particular case, if they desire to do so.

ARTICLE VIII. (1) Before a Central Body proceed to establish a Farm Colony, the Central Body shall obtain the consent of the Local Government Board.

(2) Every application by a Central Body for the consent of the Local Government Board to the establishment of a Farm Colony on land purchased by agreement, or taken on lease for that purpose, or to the establishment of a Farm Colony on land accepted by the Central Body as a donation, shall be accompanied by particulars showing:—

(i.) What is the greatest number of persons proposed to be admitted at any one time to the Farm Colony;

(ii.) What will be the arrangements for housing and maintaining the persons admitted to the Farm Colony and any officers of the Central Body;

(iii.) What is the total area of land which will be available for providing temporary work for persons admitted to the Farm Colony; and

(iv.) What part of this area comprises arable land, pasture land, land under some other form of cultivation, or uncultivated land.

(3) The Central Body shall, at the same time, furnish the Local Government Board with a statement which will give in relation to any land proposed to be acquired or to be used for the purposes of a Farm

Colony, the effect of the terms and conditions of
acquisition or use and of the covenants and customs
applicable to the land as an agricultural holding, and
which will enable the Local Government Board to
satisfy themselves that due observance of the said
terms, conditions, covenants, and customs is compatible
with the full and convenient use of the land for the
purposes of a Farm Colony.

(4) The Central Body shall likewise furnish the
Local Government Board with evidence that all expenses (other than the establishment charges of the
Central Body and their expenses in relation to the
acquisition of land) which will be incurred by the Central Body in connection with the establishment,
maintenance, and working of the Farm Colony, the
remuneration, maintenance, and accommodation of
persons employed, the payment of rates, taxes, or
assessments, or for any other purpose in relation to
the Farm Colony, may reasonably be expected to be
defrayed out of voluntary contributions, or otherwise
than out of contributions by any Council.

(1) *The Local Government Board's Observations.*

In their Circular Letter (10th October, 1905), sent with
the Regulations to London, City and Metropolitan Boroughs, the
Board made the following observations, viz. :—

"Section 4 (3) (b) of the Act enables the Board to provide
by the Regulations for authorising the establishment, with
their consent, of farm colonies by a Central Body, and Article
VIII. of the Regulations prescribes the particulars and information to be supplied to the Board when application is made to
them for their consent. The application should always be made
before the Central Body definitely undertake to establish a
farm colony.

Art. VIII.—Note—

"The acquisition of land with the consent of the Board for any of the purposes of the Act is one of the matters the cost of which can be defrayed out of the contributions of the Common Council of the City and the Metropolitan Borough Councils. Where there are buildings on the land acquired, they will, of course, pass with it, and will be taken into consideration in determining the amount of the purchase-money or of the rent, as the case may be. Where, however, there is no suitable accommodation on the land for the persons employed on the farm colony, or the accommodation is insufficient, it will be competent for the Central Body to provide the accommodation required, but the cost cannot be defrayed out of the contributions of the Councils or out of borrowed money, and must be met from other sources. *In some instances it may be practicable for the Central Body to agree with the vendor or lessor of the land that he shall provide the necessary buildings on the land. The purchase-money or the rent would be increased accordingly, and the increased purchase-money or rent might be defrayed out of the contributions of the Councils, or in the case of purchase-money, out of a Loan. The agreement might include an arrangement under which work would be given to a certain number of the unemployed in connection with the erection of the buildings.*"

In their Circular Letter of the same date, sent with the Regulations to Provincial populous Boroughs and Urban Districts the Board make the same observations, excepting that observations given above in *italics* are not—for some reason known only to the Board—included in the Provincial Circular. In this Circular Letter the "Distress Committee" are named for "Central Body" [see Article XXI.] in the London Circular Letter, and the contributions mentioned are the contributions of the Council by whom the Distress Committee are appointed. For limitations on and application of any such contributions, see Section 1 (6) of the Act.

(2) *Co-operation of one Body with another.*

The establishment of Farm Colonies are undertakings which may in some cases be best secured by a combination of Central Bodies or Distress Committees having the powers of a Central Body. This, apparently—as one matter in which combination would be advantageous—is provided for by Article XX. See Note to that Article.

(3) *Donations*—See Article XIV.
Application of Receipts of Farm Colony—See Article XV.
Acquisition of Land and Borrowing—See Articles X. and XVIII. *Also see* Article XXI.

Art. VIII.—Note—

(4) *Definition of " Farm Colonies" and purpose.*

In the House of Lords (Committee Stage) Earl Camperdown pointed out that there was no definition in the Measure of the expression "Farm Colonies." In reply, the Marquis of Lansdowne, who had charge of the Measure, said : " I take it that what is intended is that land should be acquired in the country for the purpose of teaching and promoting an interest in agricultural occupations, road-making, and such work as that. I do not think there really is any analogy, or any close analogy, between the case of a farm colony and ordinary allotments let to labourers. The farm colony experiment has, in fact, been tried with considerable success at the places to which the noble Lord referred, particularly at the farm colony established by Mr. Walter Long's Central Committee in Suffolk. The object of these farm colonies, I take it, is to provide a place which can be used as a kind of depôt for unemployed men whom it is desired to emigrate or remove to other parts of the country, and to whom it is desired to give some kind of instruction in agricultural work." [Parliamentary Debates].

Provision of temporary accommodation for workers on land.

ARTICLE IX. (1) Before a Central Body proceed to provide temporary accommodation for persons for whom the Central Body provide work upon land, the Central Body shall obtain the consent of the Local Government Board.

(2) Every application by a Central Body for the consent of the Local Government Board to the provision of temporary accommodation for persons for whom the Central Body provide work upon land shall be accompanied by plans, estimates, and particulars showing :—

(i.) The situation of the land and the nature of the work to be provided thereon ;

(ii.) The situation, nature, extent, and allocation of the temporary accommodation ;

Art. IX.

(iii.) The cost of the provision and maintenance of the temporary accommodation ; and

(iv.) Such other details as will suffice to indicate that the temporary accommodation is necessary, and will be suitable, and that the resources of the Central Body which are supplied by voluntary contributions, or otherwise than from contributions by any Council, will be adequate to defray the cost of the provision and maintenance of the temporary accommodation and all other expenses, including rates, taxes, or assessments, to be incurred in or about the provision and maintenance of the temporary accommodation.

(1) *The Observation of the Local Government Board.*

In their Circular Letter (10th October, 1905) sent with the Regulations to London, City and Metropolitan Boroughs the Board observed that:—

" The Board are further empowered by Section (4) (3) (*b*) of the Act to authorise by the Regulations the provision, with their consent, of temporary accommodation for persons for whom work upon the land is provided.

" The power given to the Central Body to provide accommodation of the kind referred to is intended to meet cases where the Central Body provide work, or contribute towards the provision of it, upon land which is too distant to enable the workmen to return home at night, and where there is no suitable accommodation available within a reasonable distance. The accommodation must be of a temporary character, and the cost cannot be defrayed out of the contributions of the Councils except in so far as it may be necessary to acquire land for the purpose.

" The Board's consent should always be obtained before the Central Body undertake to provide the accommodation."

Art. IX.—NOTE—

The same observations are contained in the Board's Circular Letter of the same date to Provincial populous Boroughs and Urban Districts. In that Circular the expression " Distress Committee " is used for the expression " Central Body " in the London Circular. [See Article XXI.]

(2) *The Adjective " Temporary."*

During the House of Lords' Committee Stage upon the Measure, Lord Balfour of Burleigh asked what was the intended interpretation of the words " Temporary Accommodation." Did the adjective " Temporary " apply to the form of the accommodation, or the time during which the occupant might remain in accommodation. The Marquis of Lansdowne, who had charge of the Measure, in reply said:—" The word may, for all I know, have both meanings attributed to it by the noble Lord, but I should say that what was contemplated was undoubtedly the temporary accommodation of unemployed persons—that is, during the time when an effort is being made to obtain employment for them." (Parliamentary Debates).

(3) [See Notes under Article VIII].

Acquisition of land

ARTICLE X. A Central Body may, with the consent of the Local Government Board, purchase by agreement or take on lease land for the purposes of the Act.

For the purpose of the purchase of land by the Central Body, the Lands Clauses Acts, except the provisions with respect to the purchase and taking of land otherwise than by agreement, and the provisions of Sections one hundred and twenty-seven to one hundred and thirty-one, and of Sections one hundred and fifty and one hundred and fifty-one of the Lands Clauses Consolidation Act, 1845, shall apply as if, subject to these Regulations, the Lands Clauses Acts except as aforesaid were incorporated with the Act, and as if for the purposes of the incorporation the Act were deemed to be the Special Act, and the Central Body were deemed to be the promoters of the undertaking:

Art. X.

Provided that nothing in the incorporated provisions of the Lands Clauses Acts or in the Act or in any Regulations made under the Act shall prevent the Central Body, on a purchase of land, from acquiring the entire fee simple free from any covenant, condition, or limitation, which would affect or interfere with the use of the land on a subsequent alienation for any purpose other than the purpose for which the land is acquired by the Central Body.

Any land acquired by a Central Body and not required for the purposes for which the land was acquired shall be disposed of and any moneys arising from the disposal shall be applied in such manner and subject to such conditions as the Local Government Board direct.

NOTE.—Article X.—

"The purposes of the Act" for which land may be acquired are the provision of temporary work which a Central Body or Distress Committee having the power of a Central Body [See Article XXI.] may provide for unemployed workmen "in proper cases" [Act, Title and Sections 1 (5) and 4 (3) *(c)*] On Article X. see Article V. and the Notes generally given to Article IX. Also Section 8 of the Act.

As to the provisions in Land Clauses Acts incorporated by Article X. see "Enactments incorporated in Regulations" following Schedule to the Regulations.

ARTICLE XI. A Distress Committee and a Central Body may each employ such officers as are necessary for the efficient exercise of the powers and the efficient discharge of the duties of the Distress Committee or Central Body.

Officers.

Note to Article XI. See Article XX.

Office
accommo-
dation.

ARTICLE XII. Where a Distress Committee or a Central Body cannot obtain the use of suitable offices belonging to a Local Authority, the Distress Committee or the Central Body may themselves provide such offices as may be necessary for their purposes.

Note to Article XII.   See Article XX.

Inspectors
at meetings.

ARTICLE XIII. An Inspector of the Local Government Board may attend every meeting of a Distress Committee, of a Central Body, or of a Special Committee; but the Inspector shall not vote at any such meeting.

NOTES. Article XIII.

Although an Inspector can not vote, his advice and assistance, however, should be of value.   It is not a new thing to give such powers as are given under this Article to an Inspector. Under the "Poor Law Board Act, 1847" (10 and 11 Vict., c. 109, s. 20), he has the rights of attending meetings of Boards of Guardians, and of taking part in the proceedings, though not of voting.   Under the "Public Health Act, 1875" (38 and 39 Vic., c. 55, s. 205), he can attend meetings of Rural and Non-Borough Urban Authorities "when, and as directed by the Local Government Board," but he has no statutory authority for taking part in the proceedings.

Donations.

ARTICLE XIV. A Central Body may accept a donation of money or other property for the purposes of the Central Body, subject to the condition that the money or other property shall be used or applied for the said purposes in such a manner as to secure compliance in all respects with the requirements of the Act and of any Regulations made under the Act, and also subject to the condition that the money or property shall not be used or applied for any other purposes; and all money or other property accepted by the Central Body shall be administered accordingly.

Art. XIV.—Note—

NOTE.—Article XIV.—

In connexion with this Regulation, Sub-section (6) of Section 1. of the Act should be referred to. All expenditure other than that provision permits to be met out of the contributions from the Councils—which are strictly limited—will have to be met by voluntary contributions, plus any receipts from Farm Colony (Article XV.) In their Circular Letters issued with the Regulations, the Local Government Board offer no opinion or make any suggestions as to methods of how voluntary contributions or donations are to be sought. It will therefore be one of the first and most important questions Central Bodies and Distress Committees having the powers of Central Bodies (Article XXI.) will have to concern themselves with. From newspaper reports it would appear that recently Mr. Keir Hardie, M.P., suggested that the restrictions in the matter of contributions from Councils, contained in Section 1. (6), might be augmented by the Councils making use of profits of Municipal Undertakings—Gas profits, &c.—as voluntary contributions for the purposes of the present Act. Clearly that could not be so, as such profits must be used in the way prescribed by the Statutory Provisions affecting the Undertakings—usually the relief of the Borough Rate.

ARTICLE XV. A Central Body shall cause all receipts arising from the working of a Farm Colony to be carried to the General Account of the Central Fund and to be afterwards transferred to the credit of the Account of Voluntary Contributions received by the Central Body.

[margin note: Receipts from Farm Colony.]

NOTE.—Article XV.

It is not simply "profit" that has to be carried to the "General Account," but *all receipts*. As to "fund" see Section 1 (6) of the Act. Also see Article XXI.

ARTICLE XVI. The Accounts of a Central Body and of the officers of the Central Body shall be made up and audited in like manner and subject to the same provisions as the accounts of a County Council and the enactments relating to the Audit of the Accounts of a

[margin note: Audit.]

Art. XVI.

County Council, and to all matters incidental thereto and consequential thereon, including the penal provisions, shall apply accordingly.

NOTE.—Article XVI.—
For the provisions incorporated in this Regulation see "Enactments incorporated in the Regulations" following the Schedule to the Regulations. Also see Article XXI.

Recovery of contributions.

ARTICLE XVII. For enforcing the payment of a contribution by a Council liable to make contributions in pursuance of the Act, sections two hundred and eighty-four and two hundred and ninety-two of the Public Health Act, 1875, shall apply as if, with the necessary modifications, they were herein re-enacted, and in terms made applicable to the payment and recovery of a contribution to be made by a Council on the demand of a Central Body.

NOTE.—Article XVII.—
For the provisions incorporated in this Regulation see "Enactments incorporated in the Regulations" following the Schedule to the Regulations. Also see Article XXI.

Borrowing.

ARTICLE XVIII. A Central Body, with the consent of the Local Government Board, may borrow money in like manner, and subject to the like conditions as a Local Authority may borrow for defraying expenses incurred in the execution of the Public Health Acts; and sections two hundred and thirty-three, two hundred and thirty-four, and two hundred and thirty-six to two hundred and thirty-nine of the Public Health Act, 1875, shall apply accordingly, with the necessary modifications, and, in particular, with the modifications herein-after set forth, that is to say:—

Art. XVIII.

      (*a*) The money shall be borrowed only for the purchase of land, and

      (*b*) The money shall be borrowed on the security of the contributions to be raised on the demand of the Central Body.

NOTE.—Article XVIII.—

For the provisions incorporated in this Regulation see "Enactments incorporated in the Regulations" following the Schedule to the Regulations. Also see Article XXI.

ARTICLE XIX. (1) Where a Local Exchange has been established within the area of a Central Body, or of a Special Committee, the Central Body or Special Committee may, by agreement, assist or take over the Local Exchange.

Labour Exchanges.

(2) Where a Central Body or a Special Committee establish a Central Exchange, the Central Body or Special Committee shall provide for the effective working, in combination with the Central Exchange, of every Local Exchange which the Central Body or Special Committee establish or assist or take over, and, so far as they may think desirable and as may be agreed, of any other Local Exchange which is within the area of the Central Body or of the Special Committee.

(3) Where two or more Central Bodies or Special Committees have established Central Exchanges, or have established or taken over Local Exchanges, those Central Bodies or Special Committees may, by agreement, co-operate for the combined working of the Central Exchanges or Local Exchanges upon such terms and subject to such conditions as may be settled by the agreement.

(4) A Central Body by whom a Local Exchange has been established or taken over may delegate the management of the Local Exchange to any Distress Committee within the area of the Central Body.

(5) A Central Body or a Special Committee may arrange for the distribution and publication of any information which, in their opinion, may prove useful to persons desirous of obtaining work.

(6) If any question or difference arises as to any proceeding or agreement, or as to any other matter or thing under this Regulation, the Local Government Board, on the application of any Central Body, Special Committee, or Local Authority concerned, and after such procedure as the Local Government Board think fit, may, by Order, determine the question or difference; and any such determination shall be final and conclusive.

(1)*The Provisions of the Act—re Labour Exchanges.*

See Sections 1 (4), 2 (1), 2 (3). Also Articles XX. and XXI.

(2) *Local Government Board's Observations.*

In their Circular Letter (10th October, 1905) to the London, City, and Metropolitan Boroughs, it is stated that:—

"The Board have not thought it expedient at the present time to make any regulations as to this matter. Should regulations be found necessary, they would of course be willing to make them, but they think that it would be desirable to obtain some experience of the working of the Act before any such regulations are made.

"The Board would not suggest that the Central Body should immediately proceed themselves to establish local labour exchanges without further information to guide them. With the view of assisting the Central Body in this matter, the Board have instructed one of their Inspectors to make inquiry as to the working of existing Labour Bureaux and to report to

Art. XIX.—Note—

them. On receipt of this Report, the Board will probably make some further communication on the subject. In the meantime they have abstained from prescribing any very detailed regulations with respect to this matter, though they have provided by Article XIX. that a Central Body by whom a Local Exchange has been established or taken over, may delegate the management of it to any Distress Committee within their area, and have also made some provision for co-operation in cases in which two or more Central Bodies or Special Committees set up under Section 2 (3) of the Act have established Central Exchanges or have established or taken over Local Exchanges.

"It will no doubt be necessary that the Central Body should establish a Central Exchange, or take over the one already established by the Central Committee of the London Unemployed Fund. If this is done, the Central Body will be required by Sub-division (2) of Article XIX. to provide for the effective working, in combination with the Central Exchange, of any Local Exchange which they establish, or assist, or take over, and, so far as they may think desirable and as may be agreed, of any other Local Exchange in London."

The same observations as in the second paragraph of the foregoing observations are contained in the Circular Letter (10th October, 1905) to Provincial populous Boroughs and Councils, "Distress Committee" being substituted for "Central Body," and in the Circular Letter (10th October, 1905) to Councils of Counties and County Boroughs under 50,000.

(3) *Forms.*

The Local Government Board have prescribed no forms for use at Labour Exchanges. Forms in use in London will be found in the Appendix, and can be easily adapted, where necessary, for any District.

(4) *Definition.*

For expression "Local Exchange" and "Central Exchange," see Article I.

(5) *General Observations.*

The provisions of the Act in relation to Labour Bureaux taken with the provisions in Article XX. are of exceedingly great importance, for, if fully worked, they permit of what has been properly termed "Industrial Clearing Houses."

J

Co-oper-
ation.

ARTICLE XX.—(1) Every Local Authority having jurisdiction in the area of a Central Body or of a Distress Committee may co-operate with or otherwise provide such assistance as the Central Body or the Distress Committee need by placing the services of an Officer of the Local Authority at the disposal of the Central Body or Distress Committee for a specified purpose, by furnishing the Central Body or Distress Committee with information in the possession of the Local Authority, or by providing the Central Body or Distress Committee with accommodation on premises belonging to the Local Authority.

Provided that, the consent of the Local Government Board shall be obtained before the services of an officer of a Poor Law Authority are placed at the disposal of a Central Body or Distress Committee.

(2) In any other case for which no provision is expressly made by these Regulations and in which it is proposed that assistance shall be provided by one Body or Committee having powers under the Act to another such Body or Committee, the several Bodies and Committees concerned may concur in framing and submitting to the Local Government Board a scheme to give effect to the proposal.

NOTE.—Article XX.—

In their Circular Letters (18th October, 1905) sent with the Regulations to London, City, and Metropolitan Boroughs, and to Provincial populous Boroughs and Urban Districts, the Local Government Board state that they hope " that Local Authorities

Art. XX.—Note—

will be willing to co-operate with the Central Body and with Distress Committees as regards officers and office accommodation. It is very desirable that expenditure on this head should be kept as low as is consistent with the efficient performance of the work of the new bodies."

On the provision made in Article XX. *re* supply of information, the Board further state that they trust "that Local Authorities will avail themselves of this provision ; " also as regards a Poor Law Authority [see definition of Board of Guardians, note Sect. 2 (2) of Act] placing services of one of their officers at disposal of Central Body, or Distress Committee, as the case may be, they say that they "will be ready to consider any application which may be made to them for their consent in any case in which the circumstances are such that the officers' services may properly be made available for the purposes of the Central Body or of a Distress Committee." [See Article XXI.]

The Local Government Board may entertain or refuse to entertain the proposal, and may, where they entertain the proposal, make such modifications in the scheme as in their opinion are necessary or expedient, and may then confirm the scheme.

ARTICLE XXI. To every Distress Committee having the powers of a Central Body these Regulations, so far as they relate to a Central Body, shall apply with the necessary adaptations, and in particular with the adaptation following, that is to say :—

Distress Committees having powers of Central Bodies.

Article X. shall have effect as if references in that Article to the Council of the Borough or Urban District were substituted for references to a Central Body.

NOTE.—Article XXI.—See Act, Section 2 (1).

Local
inquiries.

ARTICLE XXII. With respect to any proceedings of the Local Government Board under or for the purposes of the Act, subsections (1) and (5) of Section 87 of the Local Government Act 1888, shall apply with the following modification, that is to say:—

Subsection (5) shall have effect as if the Councils and other authorities therein mentioned included any Body having powers under the Act, and as if all costs payable by any such Body under the subsection as applied were thereby authorised to be defrayed as establishment charges under the Act.

NOTE.—Article XXII.—
For the provisions incorporated in this Regulation see "Enactments incorporated in the Regulations" following the Schedule to the Regulations.

Short title.

ARTICLE XXIII. These Regulations may be cited as "The Regulations (Organisation for Unemployed), 1905."

MISCELLANEOUS NOTES.

It is enacted by Section 4 (2) of the "Unemployed Workmen Act, 1905,":—"An Order of the Local Government Board under this Act may be varied and revoked by any subsequent Order of the Board made under this Act."

In connection with the Regulations contained in the preceding pages, the Local Government Board state that:— "It will probably be desirable hereafter to supplement the Regulations by some further requirements as to returns to be made to the Board, but they have not thought it expedient to deal fully with this subject at the present time." [L.G.B.C.L's. 10th October, 1905.]

SCHEDULE.

RECORD PAPER.

_____Name of Central Body. §

_____Name of Distress Committee.

No. of Application_____.   No. in Register_____

I.

1. Name of Applicant :—
   Surname   -   -   -
   Christian Names   -   -

2. Present Address in full, and Duration
   of Residence thereat   -   -

3. Preceding Address or Addresses in full,
   and Duration of Residence thereat   -

4. Age   -   -   -   -   -

5. Trade, Calling, Employment, or Occupation   -   -   -   -

6. *Condition (Married or Single, Widow
   or Widower)   -   -   -

7. Children or other Dependants :—
   Children { Number, Ages, and Sex   -
   { *Trade, Calling, Employ-
   { ment or Occupation (if any)
   Other Dependants   -   -

8. *Actual Rent and Number of Rooms in
   Applicant's tenancy   -   -
   No. of Rooms sub-let (if any)   -
   Deduct Rent for Rooms sub-let   -
   Arrears of Rent   -   -   -

Schedule.

+Here distinguish whether Applicant has been employed regularly, or, if not, at what time of the year he has been employed.

9. +Nature and Duration of Applicant's last Employment

   Full Name and Address of Employer -

   Name of Foreman

10. Date and cause of Termination of Applicant's last Employment -

11. *Rate of Wages and average Weekly Earnings received by Applicant in last Employment

12. +Particulars of other Employment of Applicant during last Five Years -

    Full Names and Addresses of Employers

    Names of Foremen

13. *Present Income of Applicant and Dependants:—

    Earnings of Applicant

    Earnings of Wife

    Earnings of Children

    Earnings of Other Dependants

    Receipts from—

       Club or Society

       Charitable Sources

       Other Sources

*If any information under this head is is contained in an original letter or other document, or in a copy attached to or inserted in the Appendix, give reference to the Appendix.

14. *Relief :—

    If no Relief has been received by Applicant or any of his Dependants -

    If Relief has been received by Applicant or any of his Dependants

       Date of last Receipt

       From what Poor Law Union

15. *Particulars of Membership, past or present, of Trade or other Provident Society

16. *Applicant's Prospect of obtaining Regular Work or other means of Supporting himself

Schedule.

17. Applicant's Fitness—
    For Work on Land in Rural Area   ·   ·
    For Change of Occupation   ·   ·
    Particulars of previous Experience (if any)

18. References to responsible Persons—
    Full Names and Addresses   ·   ·
    *Application received by _____   Date_____

II.

19. *Report (with date) on Visit and Inquiries at Applicant's Home by authorised Officer, Member or other Person -

20. *Report (with date) on Case by authorised Officer, Member, or other Person-

21. *Reports from References (if any)   ·   ·

22. Previous Record (if any) of Applicant:—
    In Record Paper retained by Distress Committee   ·   ·   ·   ·
    In Record Paper retained by Central Body ·   ·   ·   ·   ·
    In Register   ·   ·   ·   ·
    Elsewhere   ·   ·   ·   ·

23. Decision or Action on Case (with date)-

24. Record of After History of Case-
    *Statements of Applicant, verified by   Date_____

III.

APPENDIX.††

†† Here insert a copy of every letter or other document relating
to the case, or attach the original.

Given under the Seal of Office of the Local Government Board, this Tenth day of October, in the year One thousand nine hundred and five.

G. W. BALFOUR,

President.

L. S.

S. B. PROVIS,

Secretary.

ENACTMENTS INCORPORATED IN
"THE REGULATIONS (ORGANISATION FOR
UNEMPLOYED), 1905."

Acquisition of Land.—*Article X. of the Regulations.*

The expression "Lands Clauses Acts," in Article X.
of the Regulations, means: "The Land Clauses Consolidation Act, 1845; The Land Clauses Consolidation
Acts Amendment Act, 1860; The Land Clauses Consolidation Act, 1869, and The Land Clauses (Umpire)
Act, 1883, and any Acts for the time being in force
amending the same." [Interpretation Act, 1889, 52
and 53 Vict., c. 63—Sect. 23.] Since 1889 there has
been only one amending Act passed, namely, The Land
Clauses (Taxation of Costs) Act, 1895 (58 & 59 Vict.,
c. 11.) The 1845 Act was an Act passed "for consolidating in one Act certain provisions usually inserted in
Acts authorising the taking of Lands for Undertakings
of a Public Nature." It is beyond the scope of the
present work to set out at length the provisions of the
said Acts applying to acquisition of land for the pur-

poses of the Unemployed Workmen Act, 1905.   For the
information of members of Distress Committees and
Central Bodies it may, however, be pointed out:—

> (1) Land for the purposes of the Unemployed
> Workmen Act, 1905, can only be acquired by
> agreement, *i.e.*, no powers are given to compel
> owners to sell.

> (2) The Sections 127 to 131, of the Lands Clauses
> Consolidation Act, 1845 (8 Vict., c. 18) which
> Article X. of the Regulations says shall not
> apply to lands acquired for the purposes of
> the Unemployed Workmen Act, 1905, contain
> provisions for the sale of superfluous land.
> Sections 150 & 151, also made inapplicable
> by Article X., contain provisions for deposit,
> inspection, &c., of copies of Special Acts
> obtained by public bodies and companies for
> the acquisition of land, &c.

Audit.—*Article XVI. of the Regulations.*

The Statutory Provisions *re* Audit are hereunder
given—Local Government Act, 1888 (51 and 52 Vict.
c. 41).

Audit.

Section 71—(1) The accounts of the receipts and expenditure of County Councils shall be made up to the end of each local financial year, as defined by this Act, and be in the form for the time being prescribed by the Local Government Board.

Audit of Accounts of County Council.

(2) [Relates to transmission of Abstract of Accounts to Local Government Board, and to inspection of Abstract].

(3) The Accounts of a County Council, and of the County Treasurer and Officers of such Council, shall be audited by the District Auditors appointed by the Local Government Board, in like manner as Accounts of an Urban Authority and their Officers, under Sections two-hundred-and-forty-seven and two-hundred-and-fifty of the Public Health Act, 1875, and those Sections and all enactments amending them or applying to Audit by District Auditors, including the enactments imposing penalties and providing for the recovery of sums, shall apply in like manner as if, so far as they relate to an Audit of the Accounts of an Urban Authority and the Officers of such Authority, they were herein re-enacted with the necessary modifications, and accordingly all ratepayers and owners of property in the county shall have the like rights, and there shall be the same appeal as in the case of such Audit. Provided that the First Schedule to the District Auditors Act, 1879, shall be modified in manner described in the Second Schedule to this Act.

38 and 39 Vict. c. 55.

42 and 43 Vict. c. 6.

Audit.

Public Health Act (38 and 39 Vict. c. 55).
[Incorporated by Section 71 (3) of the Local
Government Act, 1888].

Section 247. Where an Urban Authority are not
the Council of a Borough, the following Regulations
with respect to audit shall be observed; (namely,)

(1) The accounts of the receipts and expenditure
under this Act of such authority shall be
audited and examined once in every year, as
soon as can be after the twenty-fifth day of
March, by the auditor of accounts relating to
the relief of the poor:

(2) [Repealed by "District Auditor's Act, 1879"].

(3) Before each audit such authority shall, after
receiving from the auditor the requisite
appointment, give at least fourteen days'
notice of the time and place at which same
will be made, and of the deposit of accounts
required by this section, by advertisement in
some one or more of the local newspapers
circulated in the district: and the production
of the newspaper containing such notice shall
be deemed to be sufficient proof of such notice
on any proceeding whatsoever:

Audit.

(4) A copy of the accounts duly made up and balanced, together with all rate books, account books, deeds, contracts, accounts, vouchers and receipts mentioned or referred to in such accounts, shall be deposited in the office of such authority, and be open, during office hours thereat, to the inspection of all persons interested for seven clear days before the audit; and all such persons shall be at liberty to take copies of or extracts from the same, without fee or reward : and any officer of such authority duly appointed in that behalf neglecting to make up such accounts and books, or altering such accounts and books, or allowing them to be altered when so made up, or refusing to allow inspection thereof, shall be liable to a penalty not exceeding five pounds :

(5) For the purpose of any audit under this Act, every auditor may, by summons in writing, require the production before him of all books, deeds, contracts, accounts, vouchers, receipts and other documents and papers which he may deem necessary, and may require any person holding or accountable for any such books, deeds, contracts, accounts, vouchers, receipts, documents or papers to appear before him at any such audit or any adjournment thereof, and to make and sign a

declaration as to the correctness of the same;
and if any such person neglects or refuses so
to do, or to produce any such books, deeds,
contracts, accounts, vouchers, receipts, documents, or papers, or to make or sign such
declaration, he shall incur for every neglect
or refusal a penalty not exceeding forty
shillings; and if he falsely or corruptly
makes or signs any such declaration, knowing
the same to be untrue in any material particular, he shall be liable to the penalties
inflicted upon persons guilty of wilful and
corrupt perjury:

(6) Any ratepayer or owner of property in the
district may be present at the audit, and may
make any objection to such accounts before
the auditor; and such ratepayers and owners
shall have the same right of appeal against
allowances by an auditor as they have by law
against disallowances:

(7) Any auditor acting in pursuance of this
section shall disallow every item of account
contrary to law, and surcharge the same on
the person making or authorising the making
of the illegal payment, and shall charge
against any person accounting the amount of
any deficiency or loss incurred by the negli-
gence or misconduct of that person, or of any

Audit.

sum which ought to have been but is not brought into account by that person, and shall in every such case certify the amount due from such person, and on application by any party aggrieved shall state in writing the reasons for his decision in respect of such disallowance or surcharge, and also of any allowance which he may have made:

(8.) Any person aggrieved by disallowance made may apply to the Court of Queen's Bench for a writ of certiorari to remove the disallowance into the said court, in the same manner and subject to the same conditions as are provided in the case of disallowances by auditors under the laws for the time being in force with regard to the relief of the poor; and the said court shall have the same powers with respect to allowances, disallowances, and surcharges under this Act as it has with respect to disallowances or allowances by the said auditors; or in lieu of such application any person so aggrieved may appeal to the Local Government Board, which Board shall have the same powers in the case of the appeal as it possesses in the case of appeals against allowances, disallowances and surcharges by the said poor law auditors:

Audit.

(9) Every sum certified to be due from any person by an auditor under this Act shall be paid by such person to the treasurer of such Authority within fourteen days after the same has been so certified, unless there is an appeal against the decision; and if such sum is not so paid, and there is no such appeal, the auditor shall recover the same from the person against whom the same has been certified to be due by the like process and with the like powers as in the case of sums certified on the audit of the poor rate accounts, and shall be paid by such Authority all such costs and expenses, including a reasonable compensation for loss of time incurred by him in such proceedings, as are not recovered by him from such person:

(10) Within fourteen days after the completion of the audit, the auditor shall report on the accounts audited and examined, and shall deliver such report to the Clerk of such Authority, who shall cause the same to be deposited in their office, and shall publish an abstract of such accounts in some one or more of the local newspapers circulated in the district.

Where the provisions as to audit of any local Act constituting a board of improvement commissioners are

Audit.

repugnant to or inconsistent with those of this Act, the audit of the accounts of such improvement commissioners shall be conducted in all respects in accordance with the provisions of this Act.

Section 249. [Relates to taxation of bill of Solicitor or Attorney.]

Section 250. The accounts under this Act of officers or assistants of any local authority who are required to receive moneys or goods on behalf of such authority shall be audited by the auditors or auditor of the accounts of such authority, with the same powers, incidents and consequences as in the case of such last-mentioned accounts.

Auditor to audit Accounts of Officers.

RECOVERY OF CONTRIBUTIONS.—*Article XVII. of the Regulations.*

The statutory provisions mentioned in the Article are as hereunder given. " Public Health Act, 1875," (38 and 39 Vict., c. 55.)

Section 284. For the purpose of obtaining payment from component districts of the sums to be contributed by them, the joint board shall issue their precept to the local authority of each component district, stating the sum to be contributed by such authority, and requiring

Payment of Contributions to Joint Board.

K

Recovery of Contributions.

such authority, within a time limited by the precept, to pay the sums therein mentioned to the joint board, or to such person as the joint board may direct.

Any sum mentioned in a precept addressed by a joint board to a local authority as aforesaid shall be a debt due from that authority, and may be recovered accordingly, such contribution in the case of a rural authority being deemed to be general expenses.

If any local authority makes default in complying with the precept addressed to it, the joint board may, instead of instituting proceedings for the recovery of a debt, or in addition to such proceedings as to any part of a debt which may for the time being be unpaid, proceed in a summary manner as in this Act mentioned to raise within the district of the defaulting authority such sum as may be sufficient to pay the sum due.

For the purpose of obtaining payment from contributory places of the sums to be contributed by them, the joint board shall have the same powers of issuing precepts and of recovering the amounts named therein as if such contributory places formed a rural district, and the joint board were the authority thereof.

Proceedings for raising a sum for payment of debt within district of a defaulting authority.

Section 292. Where any port sanitary authority, joint board, or other authority are authorised, in pursuance of this Act, to proceed in a summary manner to raise within the district of a defaulting authority such sum as may be sufficient to pay any debt due to them,

Recovery of Contributions.

the authority so authorised for the purpose of raising such sum shall, within the district of the defaulting authority, have, so far as relates to the raising such sum, the same powers as if they were the defaulting authority, and as if such sum were expenses properly incurred by the defaulting authority within the district of such authority.

Where the defaulting authority have power to raise any moneys due for their expenses by levy of a rate from individual ratepayers, the authority so authorised as aforesaid shall have power to levy such a rate by any officer appointed by them, and the officer so appointed shall have the same powers, and the rate shall be levied in the same manner and be subject to the same incidents in all respects as if it were being levied by the officer of the defaulting authority for the payment of the expenses of that authority ; and where the defaulting authority have power to raise moneys due for their expenses by issuing precepts, or otherwise requiring payments from any other authorities, the authority so authorised as aforesaid shall have the same power as the defaulting authority would have of issuing precepts, or otherwise requiring payment from such other authorities.

Any precepts issued by the authority so authorised as aforesaid for raising the sum due to them may be enforced in the same manner in all respects as if they had been issued by the defaulting authority.

Recovery of Contributions.

The authority so authorised as aforesaid may, in making an estimate of the sum to be raised for the purpose of paying the debt due to them, add such sums as they think sufficient, not exceeding ten per cent. on debt due, and may defray thereout all costs, charges and expenses (including compensation to any persons they may employ) to be incurred by such authority by reason of the default of the defaulting authority; and the authority so authorised as aforesaid shall apply all moneys raised by them in payment of the debt due to them, and such costs, charges, and expenses as aforesaid, and shall render the balance, if any, remaining in their hands after such application to the defaulting authority.

BORROWING POWERS.—*Article XVIII. of the Regulations.*

The statutory provisions mentioned in Article XVIII. are as follows. " Public Health Act, 1875 (38 and 39 Vict., c. 55).

Power to borrow on credit of rates.

Section 233. Any local authority may with the sanction of the Local Government Board for the purpose of defraying any costs, charges, and expenses incurred or to be incurred by them in the execution of the Sanitary Acts or of this Act, or for the purpose of discharging any loans contracted under the Sanitary Acts or this Act, borrow or re-borrow, and take up at interest, any sums of money necessary for defraying any such costs, charges, and expenses, or for discharging any such loans as aforesaid.

Borrowing Powers.

An Urban Authority may borrow or re-borrow any such sums on the credit of any fund or all or any rates or rate out of which they are authorised to defray expenses incurred by them in the execution of this Act, and for the purpose of securing the repayment of any sums so borrowed, with interest thereon, they may mortgage to the persons by or on behalf of whom such sums are advanced any such fund or rates or rate.

A Rural Authority may borrow or re-borrow any such sums, if applied or intended to be applied to general expenses of such authority, on the credit of the common fund out of which such expenses are payable, and if applied or intended to be applied to special expenses of such authority on the credit of any rate or rates out of which such expenses are payable, and for the purpose of securing the repayment of any sums so borrowed, with interest thereon, they may mortgage to the persons by or on behalf of whom such sums are advanced any such fund, rate or rates.

Section 234. The exercise of the powers of borrowing conferred by this Act, shall be subject to the following regulations; (namely,)

Regulations as to exercise of borrowing powers.

    (1) Money shall not be borrowed except for permanent works (including under this expression any works of which the costs ought in the opinion of the Local Government Board to be spread over a term of years):

Borrowing Powers.

(2) The sum borrowed shall not at any time
exceed, with the balances of all the out-
standing loans contracted by the local authority under the Sanitary Acts and this Act, in
the whole the assessable value for two years
of the premises assessable within the district
in respect of which such money may be
borrowed :

(3) Where the sum proposed to be borrowed with
such balances (if any) would exceed the
assessable value for one year of such premises,
the Local Government Board shall not give
their sanction to such loan until one of their
inspectors has held a local inquiry and
reported to the said board :

(4) The money may be borrowed for such time,
not exceeding sixty years, as the local authority, with the sanction of the Local Government Board, determine in each case; and,
subject as aforesaid, the local authority shall
either pay off the moneys so borrowed by
equal annual instalments of principal or of
principal and interest, or they shall in every
year set apart as a sinking fund, and accumulate in the way of compound interest by
investing the same in the purchase of Ex-

Borrowing Powers.

chequer bills or other Government securities, such sum as will with accumulations in the way of compound interest be sufficient, after payment of all expenses, to pay off the moneys so borrowed within the period sanctioned :

(5) A local authority may at any time apply the whole or any part of a sinking fund set apart under this Act in or towards the discharge of the moneys for the repayment of which the fund has been established: Provided that they pay into the fund in each year and accumulate until the whole of the moneys borrowed are discharged, a sum equivalent to the interest which would have been produced by the sinking fund or the part of the sinking fund so applied :

(6) Where money is borrowed for the purpose of discharging a previous loan, the time for repayment of the money so borrowed shall not extend beyond the unexpired portion of the period for which the original loan was sanctioned, unless with the sanction of the Local Government Board, and shall in no case be extended beyond the period of sixty years from the date of the original loan.

Borrowing Powers.

Where any urban authority borrow any money for the purpose of defraying private improvement expenses, or expenses in respect of which they have determined a part only of the district to be liable, it shall be the duty of such authority, as between the ratepayers of the district, to make good, so far as they can, the money so borrowed, as occasion requires, either out of private improvement rates, or out of a rate levied in such part of the district as aforesaid.

Section 236.   [Deals with Form of Mortgage.]

Section 237.   [Register of Mortgages to be kept, and to be open to public inspection during office hours, without fee or reward.]

Section 238.   [Deals with Transfer of Mortgages.]

Section 239.   [Contains provision for appointment of Receiver on non-payment of principal money or interest on Mortgage of Rates.]

LOCAL INQUIRIES.—*Article XXII. of the Regulations.*

The statutory provisions mentioned in the Article are as follows. "Local Government Act, 1888" (51 and 52 Vict., c. 41).

Local Inquiries.

Section 87. (1) Where the Local Government Board are authorized by this Act to make an inquiry, to determine any difference, to make or confirm any order, to frame any scheme, or to give any consent, sanction, or approval to any matter, or otherwise to act under this Act, they may cause to be made a local inquiry, and in that case, and also in a case where they are required by this Act to cause to be made a local inquiry, sections two-hundred-and-ninety-three to two-hundred-and-ninety-six, both inclusive, of "The Public Health Act, 1875," shall apply as if they were herein re-enacted, and in terms made applicable to this Act.

Section 87. (5) Where the board cause any local inquiry to be held under this Act, the costs incurred in relation to such inquiry, including the salary of any inspector or officer of the Board engaged in such inquiry, not exceeding three guineas a day, shall be paid by the councils and other authorities concerned in such inquiry, or by such of them and in such proportions as the Board may direct, and the Board may certify the amount of the costs incurred, and any sum so certified and directed by the Board to be paid by any council or authority shall be a debt to the Crown from such council or authority.

Application of provisions of 38 and 39 Vict., c 55, as to local inquiries and provisional orders.

Sections 293 to 296 of the Public Health Act, 1875,
(38 and 39 Vict. c. 55).

[Incorporated in Section 87 (1) of the Local Government
Board Act, 1888 (above given).]

———————

Power of
Board to
direct
inquiries.

Section 293. The Local Government Board may
from time to time cause to be made such inquiries as
are directed by this Act, and such inquiries as they see
fit in relation to any matters concerning the public
health in any place, or any matters with respect to
which their sanction, approval, or consent is required
by this Act.

Order as to
cost of
inquiries.

Section 294. The Local Government Board may
make orders as to the costs of inquiries or proceedings
instituted by, or of appeals to, the said Board under
under this Act, and as to the parties by whom or the
rates out of which such costs shall be borne; and every
such order may be made a rule of one of the superior
courts of law on the application of any person named
therein.

Orders of
Board
under this
Act.

Section 295. All orders made by the Local Government Board in pursuance of this Act shall be binding
and conclusive in respect of the matters to which they
refer, and shall be published in such manner as that
Board may direct.

Local Inquiries.

Section 296.   Inspectors of the Local Government
Board shall, for the purposes of any inquiry directed by
the Board, have in relation to witnesses and their
examination, the production of papers and accounts,
and the inspection of places and matters required to
be inspected, similar powers to those which Poor Law
Inspectors have under the Acts relating to the relief of
the poor for the purposes of these Acts.

Powers of
Inspectors
of Local
Government Board.

NOTE.—Poor Law Inspectors have powers to summon any
persons before them, and to examine witnesses on oath ; to
call for the production of contracts, agreements, accounts, etc.
To disobey an Inspector is a misdemeanour; to give false
evidence is perjury.   [Poor Law Board Act, 1847 (10 and 11
Vict., c. 109, S. 21).]

LABOUR EXCHANGES AND THEIR CO-ORDINATION.

LABOUR BUREAUX (LONDON) ACT, 1902.

(2 Edw. VII., Ch. 13.)

CHAPTER XIII.

An Act to authorise the establishment of Labour Bureaux throughout the Metropolis.   [22nd July, 1902.]

BE it enacted by the King's most Excellent Majesty, by and with the advice and consent of the Lords Spiritual and Temporal, and Commons, in this present Parliament assembled, and by the authority of the same, as follows :—

1. It shall be lawful for the council of any metropolitan borough to establish and maintain a labour bureau.

2. Any expenses incurred by a borough council in or incidental to the exercise of the powers conferred by this Act shall be paid out of the general rate.

3. In this Act the term "labour bureau" shall mean an office or place used for the purpose of supplying information either by the keeping of registers or otherwise respecting employers who desire to engage workpeople and workpeople who seek engagement or employment.

4. This Act may be cited as the Labour Bureau (London) Act, 1902.

NOTE.—The Metropolitan Boroughs, where a Labour Bureau has been established under the provisions of the above Act, are:—Battersea, Chelsea, Finsbury, Fulham, Hammersmith, Hampstead, Islington, Kensington, Poplar, St. Pancras, Southwark, Stepney, Westminster.

The "Unemployed Workmen Act, 1905" (5 Edw. 7, c. 18) is the first general Statute to make provision for the establishment of Labour Exchanges. It is a fact, however, that outside London, during recent years "Labour Bureaux have in some Boroughs been established by the Borough Council, and there are others which have been set up by other bodies," [L.G.B.C.L. with Regulations to Councils of populous Boroughs and Urban Districts in the provinces (10th October, 1905)].

EMPLOYMENT EXCHANGES AND
THEIR CO-ORDINATION.

EXTRACT from "Preliminary Statement (as on the 14th of April, 1905) prepared at the request of the President of the Local Government Board by the Central Executive Committee" of the "Organisation known as the London Unemployed Fund," which had its origin in a scheme proposed at conference of Metropolitan Guardians by the Right Hon. W. H. Long, M.P., then President of the Local Government Board, on October 14th, 1904.

"The co-ordination of the existing Bureaux, through the medium of a Central Employment Exchange, was felt to be the most hopeful step for achieving this aim. Accordingly, as far back as December 22nd, the formation of such an Exchange was recommended, and the step having been approved by the Executive Committee, a Conference bringing the proposal to the notice of those likely to be interested and to elicit suggestions, was held on January 26th. To this Conference the Chairmen of the Committees of Management of the existing Exchanges and their Superintendents were invited, and as the sequel to a well-attended meeting a Consultative Committee of those actually engaged in the working of the Exchanges was appointed to meet and confer with the Classification Committee—an experiment that has been entirely successful.

"In order to aid in the formation of local Exchanges in the future, and with a view to providing a uniform standard of work among them, a set of model rules and application forms has been adopted, and many other points of administration have been discussed and decided upon. So far, however, the most important step taken has been to inaugurate the working of the new Central Exchange, the offices for which were taken in March in Victoria Street, Westminster. Mr. H. W. Fordham, lately in charge of the Fulham Employment Exchange, has been appointed Superintendent, and a systematic plan of co-operation is being rapidly developed. It is too early to report as to results, but at the present time the Central Exchange is being used by seven (*since considerably increased*) of the Local Exchanges. For these and for all that use it in the future, the Central Exchange will thus provide a ready means of inter-communication, and through it, whenever applicants cannot be provided with employment, or places cannot be filled locally, the attempt can be made by working over a larger area, to adjust the balance.

"The Central Exchange is the inception of what may become not only one of the more permanent outcomes of the work of the winter, but one of the greatest utility. Its functions will be to increase the fluidity of labour; to provide a new instrument by which wage-earners may be enabled to find the billets that they need and employers the men they want, while, incidentally, it will increase knowledge of the prevailing conditions of employment,

"The Exchange is intended. to quote from the model Application Form, to 'aid applicants in their search for work, and not to take the place of their own efforts.' It will thus, in every respect, work through ordinary channels, and its institutition is another recognition of the supreme importance of maintaining and strengthening the normal courses of industry."

MODEL RULES AND FORMS.

The Model Rules and Forms adopted as stated in the foregoing extract are as herein given:—

EMPLOYMENT EXCHANGE.

(Affiliated to the Central Employment Exchange.)

Rules Suggested by the Central Committee.

1. The Exchange will be opened for men daily from   , and for women from   , except Saturdays. The Exchange will be closed on Good Friday, Christmas Day, Bank Holidays, and on any occasion the   may see fit to notify.

2. Only persons resident in the Borough of   at the time of application can be registered for employment; but this restriction as to residence does not apply to employers of labour.

3. Every applicant for registration shall either fill up correctly a printed form, obtainable on personal application to the superintendent, or answer such questions as shall be put by the superintendent, for the purpose of enabling him to enter the necessary particulars in the register.

L.

4. The Superintendent will recommend applicants for employment according to suitability, but employers may select from the registered applicants any one whom they consider suitable.

5. Only those out of employment, or under notice of discharge, will be registered.

6. The name of every applicant will be removed from the register after one month, exclusive of Sundays and public holidays, unless the applicant, on or before the end of the month, gives notice that he or she is still out of employment, such notice to be repeated not less often than on every succeeding month that the applicant remains out of employment.

7. Applicants must notify the Superintendents when they obtain employment through the Exchange.

FORM OF APPLICATION.

Metropolitan Borough of
Municipal Employment Exchange.

(Affiliated with the Central Employment Exchange).

Address_____ Office Hours_____

No. _____ Date_____

Name_____

Address_____

Married or Single.	What family.	How long resident in the Borough.

Exact description of employment required.	Other work for which qualified.

Name and Address of last Employer and description of work.

Name and Address of longest Employer and description of work.

What Sick Benefit, Trade, or other Society are you a member of?

Any remarks.

For the sake of other applicants please inform the Superintendent immediately you obtain work, whether temporary or permanent.

N.B.—Employment cannot be guaranteed. This exchange is intended to aid applicants in their search for work, and not to take the place of their own efforts.

NOTE.—Where offices of Distress Committee and Labour Exchange are combined, the foregoing Form may not be considered necessary seeing that application has to be entered on "Record Paper," given in the Schedule of "The Regulations (Organisation for Unemployed), 1905."

Card of Introduction of Unemployed Workmen to Employer.

Metropolitan Borough of
MUNICIPAL EMPLOYMENT EXCHANGE.
TOWN HALL, HIGH STREET.

NO FEES. 190

To ....

....

Re

Dear Sir,

In reply to your advertisement in the ....

of .... *may I introduce bearer* ....

of .... *who is seeking work in above position?*

No fees whatever are charged for this introduction.

Yours faithfully,

OVER] *Superintendent.*

[BACK OF CARD.]

EMPLOYERS are informed that every endeavour will be made to suit them at short notice with :—

Carmen, Chauffeurs, Mechanics, Handy-men, Porters, Messengers, Caretakers, General Labourers, Travellers, Clerks, Shorthand Writers and Typists, Shop Assistants, Waiters and Waitresses, Domestic Servants, Girls, Boys, Youths, etc., etc.

NO FEES WHATEVER.

Office Hours.—8-0 till 4-0.   Telephone No.

Saturdays.—8-0 till 12-0.   Superintendent.

Post Card to Unemployed Applicant to call at Registry.

Metropolitan Borough of

MUNICIPAL EMPLOYMENT EXCHANGE.

TOWN HALL, HIGH STREET.

Telephone No.

190

With reference to your application for employment.
if you are still disengaged please call _____
next, at _____ o'clock sharp.

SUPERINTENDENT.

Post Card stating that Employment has been Obtained.

Metropolitan Borough of

MUNICIPAL EMPLOYMENT EXCHANGE,

TOWN HALL, HIGH STREET.

Telephone No.

REGISTRY AND EMPLOYMENT CARD.

Registered No. _____
Date of Removal _____

Sir, I have obtained employment with _____

This Card must be brought to the Registry at least every Seven Days, if out of work. On obtaining employment, whether permanent or temporary, send this Card immediately to the Registry.

[On Address Side—Postal Address of Superintendent of Exchange is printed.]

Form of Exchange Daily Register.

Metropolitan Borough of_____Municipal Employment Exchange.

Date_____

Register No.	NAME.	Address.	Age.	Employment Required.	Last Employer.	Sick, Trade, or Benefit Society.	Remarks.

This is in Book Form of Double Foolscap, and contains 12 lines to the sheet.

Model Rules and Forms.

FORM OF DAILY RETURN.

From Superintendent of Borough Labour Exchange to Superintendent of Central Exchange.

The Central Employment Exchange,

34, Victoria Street, Westminster, S.W.

Report from the Borough

of .... *Date* ....

The following have registered as Unemployed this day.

Signed ....

[Here follows printed list of Trades and Callings.]

FORM OF WEEKLY RETURN MADE BY BOROUGH EXCHANGE.

𝔐etropolitan 𝔅orough of
MUNICIPAL EMPLOYMENT EXCHANGE.

During the Week ended .... 1905.

	MALES.	FEMALES.
Fresh Applications	...	...
Renewals	...	...
TOTAL.........		

Statement showing the Number of each Class of Workers Registered and Engaged during the Week.

DIVISIONS OF LABOUR ON REGISTER	MALES.		FEMALES.	
	Reg.	Eng.	Reg.	Eng.
[Here follows Printed List of Trades and Callings.]				
TOTAL..............				

	MALES.	FEMALES.
Number of Persons who have secured Employment during the week through this Agency		...
Number of Employers who have called or written during the week in want of Employees		...

.... *Superintendent.*

FORMS OF MEMOS IN USE AT THE EXCHANGE.

190

DEAR SIR,

    I can place the following: —

    Please let the applicants apply to

                    Yours faithfully,

190

DEAR SIR,

    I am happy to state that in consequence of information from THE CENTRAL EMPLOYMENT EXCHANGE I have been able to place

              Yours faithfully,

THE OUT-DOOR RELIEF ORDERS.

The Regulations of the Poor Law Commissioners (now the Local Government Board) relating to Out-door Relief are contained in two orders, viz. "The Out-door Relief Prohibitory Order," and the "Out-door Relief Regulation Order." The "Prohibitory" Order is in operation in over three-fourths of the Unions. The "Regulation" Order is in operation in the other Unions, which include the Unions of dense populations. Distress Committees should satisfy themselves as to which Order is in operation in their areas respectively.

The question of who or who is not able-bodied is one of fact, and not of age. At the time of the issue of the Orders, Out-Relief was a parish charge, now it is a Union charge.

The two Orders are given hereunder :—

OUT-DOOR RELIEF PROHIBITORY ORDER.

Issued by the Poor Law Commissioners (now the Local Government Board) 21st December, 1844.

ARTICLE I. Every able-bodied person, male or female, requiring relief from any Parish within any of the said Unions, shall be relieved only in the Workhouse

Article I.

of the Union, together with such of the family of every such able-bodied person as may be resident with him or her, and may not be in employment, and together with the wife of every such able-bodied male person, if he be a married man and if she be resident with him; save and except the following cases :—

> 1st. Where such person shall require relief on account of sudden and urgent necessity.
>
> 2nd. Where such person shall require relief on account of any sickness, accident or bodily or mental infirmity affecting such person, or any of his or her family.
>
> 3rd. Where such person shall require relief for the purpose of defraying the expenses, either wholly or in part, of the burial of any of his or her family.
>
> 4th. Where such person, being a widow shall be in the first six months of her widowhood.
>
> 5th. Where such person shall be a widow, and have a legitimate child or legitimate children dependent upon her, and incapable of earning his, her, or their livelihood, and have no illegitimate child born after the commencement of her widowhood.
>
> 6th. Where such person shall be confined in any gaol or place of safe custody, subject always to the regulation contained in Article 4.

7th. Where such person shall be the wife, or child, of any able-bodied man who shall be in the service of His Majesty as a soldier, sailor, or marine.

8th. Where any able-bodied person, not being a soldier, sailor, or marine, shall not reside within the Union, but the wife, child, or children of such person shall reside within the same, the Board of Guardians of the Union, according to their discretion, may, subject to the regulation contained in Article IV., afford relief in the Workhouse to such wife, child, or children, or may allow out-door relief for any such child or children being within the age of nurture, and resident with the mother within the Union.

ARTICLE II.   In every case in which out-door relief shall be given on account of sickness, accident, or infirmity to any able-bodied male person resident within any of the said Unions, or to any member of the family of any able-bodied male person, an extract from the Medical Officer's Weekly Report (if any such Officer shall have attended the case), stating the nature of such sickness, accident, or infirmity, shall be specially entered in the Minutes of the Proceedings of the Board of Guardians of the day on which the relief is ordered or subsequently allowed.

Article II.

But if the Board of Guardians shall think fit, a certificate under the hand of a Medical Officer of the Union, or of the Medical Practitioner in attendance on the party, shall be laid before the Board, stating the nature of such sickness, accident, or infirmity, and a copy of the same shall be in like manner entered in the Minutes.

ARTICLE III. No relief shall be given from the poor-rates of any parish comprised in any of the said Unions to any person who does not reside in some place within the Union, save and except in the following cases :—

1st. Where such person, being casually within such parish, shall become destitute.

2nd. Where such person shall require relief on account of any sickness, accident, or bodily or mental infirmity, affecting such person, or any of his or her family.

3rd. Where such person shall be entitled to receive relief from any parish in which he or she may not be resident, under any order which Justices may by law be authorized to make.

4th. Where such person, being a widow, shall be in the first six months of her widowhood.

5th. Where such person is a widow, who has a legitimate child dependent on her for support, and no illegitmate child born after the commencement of her widowhood, and who at the time of her husband's death was resident with him in some place other than the parish of her legal settlement, and not situated in the Union in which such parish may be comprised.

6th. Where such person shall be a child under the age of sixteen, maintained in a Workhouse or Establishment for the education of pauper children not situate within the Union.

7th. Where such person shall be the wife or child residing within the Union, of some person not able-bodied, and not residing within the Union.

8th. Where such person shall have been in the receipt of relief from some parish in the Union from which such person seeks relief, at some time within the twelve calendar months next preceding the date of that one of the several Orders hereinbefore recited which was applicable to that Union, being settled in such parish, and not being resident within the Union at the time of the allowance of the relief.

ARTICLE IV. Where the husband of any woman is beyond the seas, or in custody of the law, or in confinement in a licensed house or asylum as a lunatic or idiot, all relief which the Guardians shall give to his wife, or her child or children, shall be given to such woman in the same manner, and subject to the same conditions, as if she were a widow.

ARTICLE V. It shall not be lawful for the Guardians, or any of their Officers, or for the Overseer or Overseers of any parish in the Union to pay, wholly or in part, the rent of the house or lodging of any pauper, or to apply any portion of the relief ordered to be given to any pauper in payment of any such rent, or to retain any portion of such relief for the purpose of directly or indirectly discharging such rent, in full or in part, for any such pauper.

Provided always, that nothing in this Article contained shall apply to any shelter or temporary lodging, procured in any case of sudden and urgent necessity, or mental imbecility, or shall be taken to prevent the said Guardians, in regulating the amount of relief to be afforded to any particular person, from considering the expense to be incurred by such person in providing lodging.

ARTICLE VI. Provided always, that in case the Guardians of any of the said Unions depart in any particular instance from any of the regulations hereinbefore contained, and within fifteen days after such departure report the same, and the grounds thereof, to the Poor Law Commissioners, and the Poor Law Commissioners approve of such departure, then the relief granted in such particular instance shall, if otherwise lawful, not be deemed to be unlawful, or be subject to be disallowed.

ARTICLE VII.   No relief which may be contrary to any regulation in this Order shall be given by way of loan; and any relief which may be given to, or on account of, any person above the age of twenty-one, or to his wife, or any part of his or her family under the age of sixteen, under Article I., or any of the exceptions thereto, or under any of the exceptions to Article III., or under Article IV., or under the proviso in Article VI., may, if the Guardians think fit, be given by way of loan.

ARTICLE VIII.   Whenever the word "Parish" is used in this Order, it shall be taken to include any place separately, maintaining its own poor, whether parochial or extra-parochial.

ARTICLE IX.   Whenever the word "Union" is used in this Order, it shall be taken to include not only an Union of Parishes formed under the provisions of the hereinbefore recited Act, but also any Union of Parishes incorporated or united for the relief or maintenance of the poor under any Local Act of Parliament.

ARTICLE X.   Whenever the word "Guardians" is used in this Order, it shall be taken to include not only Guardians appointed or entitled to act under the provisions of the said hereinbefore recited Act, but also any Governors, Directors, Managers, or Acting Guardians entitled to act in the ordering of relief to the poor from the poor-rates under any Local Act of Parliament.

ARTICLE XI. Whenever in this Order any Article is referred to by its number, the Article of this Order bearing that number shall be taken to be signified thereby.

OUT-DOOR RELIEF REGULATION ORDER

(*Dated 14th December*, 1852).

ARTICLE I. Whenever the Guardians allow relief to any able bodied male person, out of the Workhouse, one half at least of the relief so allowed shall be given in articles of food or fuel, or in other articles of absolute necessity.

ARTICLE II. In any case in which the Guardians allow relief for a longer period than one week to an indigent poor person, resident within their Union or Parish respectively, without requiring that such person shall be received into the Workhouse, such relief shall be given or administered weekly, or at such more frequent periods as they may deem expedient.

ARTICLE III. It shall not be lawful for the Guardians or their officers

> To establish any applicant for relief in trade or business;
>
> Nor to redeem from pawn for any such applicant any tools, implements, or other articles;
>
> Nor to purchase and give to such applicant any tools, implements, or other articles, except articles of clothing or bedding where urgently needed, and such articles as are hereinbefore referred to in Article I;

M

Nor to pay, directly or indirectly, the expense of the conveyance of any poor person, unless conveyed under the provisions of some Statute, or under an Order of Justices or other lawful authority or in conformity with some Order or Regulation of the Poor Law Commissioners or the Poor Law Board, except in the following cases; viz.—

ARTICLE III.   1st. The case of a person conveyed to or from a district school, or an hospital or infirmary, or a lunatic asylum, or a house licensed or hospital registered for the reception of lunatics;

2nd. The case of a person conveyed to the Workhouse of the Union or Parish in which such person is at the time chargeable;

3rd. The case of a person conveyed to or from any other Workhouse or other house or establishment for the reception of poor persons, in which for the time being it shall be lawful for the Guardians to place such person;

Nor to give money to or on account of any such applicant for the purpose of affecting any of the objects in this Article mentioned;

Nor to pay, wholly or in part, the rent of the house or lodging of any pauper, nor to apply any portion of the relief ordered to be given to any pauper in payment of any such rent,

Art. III.

nor to retain any portion of such relief for the purpose of directly or indirectly discharging such rent, in full or in part, for any such pauper;

Provided always, that nothing in this Article contained shall apply to any shelter or temporary lodging procured for a poor person in any case of sudden or urgent necessity or mental imbecility.

ARTICLE IV. No relief shall be given from the poor-rates of any of the said Parishes, or of any Parish comprised in any of the said Unions, to any person who does not reside in some place within such Parish or Union respectively, save and except in the following cases:—

1st. The case of a person casually within such Parish, and destitute.

2nd. The case of a person requiring relief on account of any sickness, accident, or bodily or mental infirmity, affecting him or her, or any of his or her family.

3rd. The case of a widow, having a legitimate child dependent on her for support, and no illegitimate child born after the commencement of her widowhood, and who at the time of her husband's death was resident with him in some place other than the Parish of her legal settlement, and not situated in the Union in which such Parish is comprised.

4th. The case of a child under the age of sixteen maintained in a Workhouse or establishment for the education of poor children not situate within the Union or Parish.

5th. The case of the wife or child residing within such Parish or Union of some person not residing therein.

6th. The case of a person who has been in the receipt of relief from such Parish, or from some Parish in the Union from which he or she seeks relief, at some time within the twelve calendar months next preceding the date of this Order.

ARTICLE V. No relief shall be given to any able-bodied male person while he is employed for wages or other hire or remuneration by any person.

ARTICLE VI. Every able-bodied male person, if relieved out of the Workhouse, shall be set to work by the Guardians, and be kept employed under their direction and superintendence so long as he continues to receive relief.

ARTICLE VII. Provided that the regulations in Articles V. and VI. shall not be imperative in the following cases :—

1st. The case of a person receiving relief on account of sudden and urgent necessity.

Art. VII.

> 2nd. The case of a person receiving relief on account of any sickness, accident, or bodily or mental infirmity, affecting such person or any of his family.
>
> 3rd. The case of a person receiving relief for the purpose of defraying the expenses of the burial of any of his family.
>
> 4th. The case of the wife, child, or children of a person confined in any gaol, or place of safe custody.
>
> 5th. The case of the wife, child, or children, resident within the Parish or Union of a person not residing therein.

ARTICLE VIII. The Guardians shall, within thirty days after they shall have proceeded to act in execution of Article VI., report to the Poor Law Board the place or places at which able-bodied male paupers shall be set to work, the sort or sorts of work in which they or any of them shall be employed, the times and mode of work, and the provision made for superintending them while working, and shall forthwith discontinue or alter the same, if the Poor Law Board shall so require.

ARTICLE IX. No relief which shall be contrary to any regulation in this Order shall be given by way of loan, but any relief which may be given in conformity with the provisions of this Order to or on account of any person to whom relief may be lawfully given above the age of twenty-one, or to his wife, or any part of his or her family under the age of sixteen, may, if the Guardians shall think fit, be given by way of loan.

ARTICLE X.   If the Guardians shall, upon consideration of the special circumstances of any particular case, deem it expedient to depart from any of the Regulations hereinbefore contained (except those contained in Article III.), and within twenty-one days after such departure shall report the same, and the grounds thereof, to the Poor Law Board, the relief which may have been so given in such case by such Guardians before an answer to such report shall have been returned by the said Board, shall not be deemed to be contrary to the provisions of this Order, and if the Poor Law Board shall approve of such departure, and shall notify such approval to the Guardians, all relief given in such case after such notification, so far as the same shall be in accordance with the terms and conditions of such approval, shall be lawful, anything in this Order to the contrary notwithstanding.

ARTICLE XI.   Whenever the word "Guardians" is used in this Order it shall be taken to include not only Guardians appointed or entitled to act, under the provisions of the said hereinbefore recited Act, but also any Governors, Directors, Managers, Acting Guardians, Vestrymen, or other Officers in a Parish or Union, appointed or entitled to act as Managers of the Poor, and in the distribution or ordering of the relief of the Poor from the poor-rate, under any general or local Act.

ARTICLE XII.   Whenever the word "Parish" is used in this Order, it shall be taken to include any place separately maintaining its own Poor, whether parochial or extra-parochial.

ARTICLE XIII. Whenever in describing any person or party, matter, or thing, the word importing the singular number only is used in this Order, the same shall be taken to include, and shall be applied to several persons or parties as well as one person or party, and several matters or things as well as one matter or thing respectively, unless there be something in the subject or context repugnant to such construction.

ARTICLE XIV. Whenever in this Order any Article is referred to by its number, the Article of this Order bearing that number shall be taken to be signified thereby.

INDEX.

PAGE

Register of Cases to be kept by D.C. and C.B. 116
Removal to another Area—see "Migration."
Removal of Difficulties—see "Difficulties."
Remuneration of Workman—see under "Workman."
Resignation—see under "Distress Committee" and "Central Body."
Returns to L.G.B. 32
  ,, to L.G.B. of cases emigrated 105

Scheme, see "Local Government Board" ... ...
Scotland, application of Act to 33
Special Committee, in county boroughs *re* labour exchanges, &c. 26
  ,, in administrative counties   ,, 26
  ,, expenses of 26
  ,, powers of 26, 127
  ,, constitution of as temporary C.B. or D.C. ... 28
  ,, may arrange for distribution of employment
      information 128

Statutes :
  Poor Law Relief Act, 1601, ...s. 7, 96
  Poor Law Amendment Act, 1834, 25 ; ss. 57 to 71, 96 ; s. 56, 98
  Land Clauses Consolidation Act, 1845... ... 138 ; s. 127, 131
  Land Clauses Acts 137
  Poor Removal Act, 1846 ... ... s. 6, 106
  Lord Campbell's Act, 1846 96
  Poor Law Board Act, 1847 ... ... s. 20, 124 ; s. 21, 155
  Union Chargeability Act, 1865 ... ... s. 8, 101
  Metropolitan Poor Act, 1867 ... ... s. 11, 54
  Vaccination Act, 1867 ... ... s. 26, 23
  Poor Law Amendment Act, 1868 ... ... s. 37, 96
  Naturalization Act, 1870 61
  Bastardy Law Amendment Act, 1872... ... ... s. 4, 96
  Public Health Act, 1875, s. 205, 124 ; s. 233, 148, 9 ; s. 234,
    149 ; ss. 236 to 9, 152 ; s. 247, 146 to 5 ; ss. 249, 250,
    —145-6 ; s. 292, 146 to 148 ; ss. 293, 4, 5—154 ; s. 296,
                             155 ; schedule II., 62
  Elementary Education Act, 1876 ... ... s. 10, 22
  District Auditors' Act, 1879 140
  Municipal Corporations Act, 1882 ... ... s. 33, 23 ; s. 22, 65
  Married Women's Property Act, 1882 ... ... ss. 20, 21, 96
  Medical Relief Disqualification Removal Act, 1885 23 ; s. 4, 99
  Local Government Act, 1888— 25
  Mortmain and Charitable Uses Act, 1888—
       s. 71, 138, 9 ; s. 87, 153 ; ss. 1 & 100, 25
  Interpretation Act, 1889—
       s. 1, 96 ; s. 3, 101 ; s. 15, 25 ; s. 16, 25 ; s. 23, 127
  Mortmain and Charitable Uses Act, 1891 ... ...s. 3, 54
  Public Health (in London) Act, 1891... ... ... s. 80, 23

Lightning Source UK Ltd.
Milton Keynes UK
UKOW06f2235250913

217968UK00011B/554/P